THE HOLMES INSPECTION

MIKE HOLMES

EVERYTHING YOU NEED TO KNOW
BEFORE YOU BUY OR SELL YOUR HOME

The Holmes Inspection
Text © 2012, 2008 by Restovate Ltd.
All rights reserved.

First edition

Copyright © 2012 Time Home Entertainment Inc.

Published by Time Home Entertainment Inc.
135 West 50th Street
New York, New York 10020

Published by arrangement with HarperCollins Publishers Ltd.

ISBN 10: 1-60320-929-8; ISBN 13: 978-1-60320-929-8

We welcome your comments and suggestions about Time Home Entertainment Inc. Books.
Please write to us at:
Time Home Entertainment Inc. Books
Attention: Book Editors
PO Box 11016
Des Moines, IA 50336-1016

If you would like to order any of our hardcover Collector's Edition books, please call us at 1-800-327-6388. (Monday through Friday, 7:00 a.m.— 8:00 p.m. or Saturday, 7:00 a.m.— 6:00 p.m. Central Time).

Printed and bound in the United States

Holmes, Mike
The Holmes inspection : everything you need to know
before you buy or sell your home / Mike Holmes.

1. Dwellings—Inspection—Amateurs' manuals.
2. House buying. I. Title.

TH4817.5.H645 2008   643'.12   C2007-906586-4

P+ 9 8 7 6 5 4 3 2 1

All photographs © 2008 Joseph Marranca, except the following:
Courtesy of American Standard 139, 147; The Holmes Group i, ii, 7, 11, 13, 27, 51, 85, 92, 95, 110, 128, 146, 153; istockphoto 73; M. Eric Honeycutt/istockphoto 10; Oksana Struk/istockphoto 30; Branko Miokovic/istockphoto 31; Stan Rohrer/istockphoto 29 (top); Margaret Cooper/istockphoto 33 (bottom); Rich Legg/istockphoto 33, 42; Matej Michelizza/istockphoto 49 (bottom); Andy Piatt/istockphoto 49 (top); Radoslaw Kostka/istockphoto 50 (bottom left); Gary Martin/istockphoto 53; Paige Falk/istockphoto 54 (bottom); Donald Swartz/istockphoto 65; Pierrette Guertin/istockphoto 66; Paul Clarke/istockphoto 69; Dave Logan/istockphoto 74; Steven Miric/istockphoto 75 (top); Karen Keczmerski/istockphoto 104; Ronnie Comeau/istockphoto 119 (top left); Bojan Pavlukovic/istockphoto 119 (top right); Bill Noll/istockphoto 119 (bottom left); Lya Cattel/istockphoto 119 (bottom right); Courtesy of Jeld-Wen vi, Exterior tab (facing 37); courtesy of Mills Pride 137, 143

Illustrations by Imagineering Media Services

FOR MY DAD

CONTENTS

INTRODUCTION

WHY IS IT NORMAL FOR HOME INSPECTIONS TO FAIL?

My dad always said to me, "Mike, never take advantage of people. Be honest. Keep your word and always do it right the first time." And that has always stuck with me — that's what should be "normal" in everything you do.

But that's not what's normal for far too many people when they're buying or selling or having work done on a home. I get over a thousand emails every week from people who have serious problems with their homes: basements flooding, foundations sinking, additions without insulation, plumbing and electrical issues galore. But the No. 1 complaint — by a long shot — comes from people who discover major issues that their home inspector should have caught.

Home inspectors are not spotting the red flags right there in front of their eyes. And sellers are not always being honest about their houses, instead covering up problems or passing them along to unsuspecting buyers. In one house I inspected for this book, for example, the sellers not only covered over structural issues, they introduced a whole lot more problems when they renovated the house for a quick "flip." There are so many issues that it will cost at least $150,000 to fix everything — in a $300,000 house that was passed by a home inspector.

Who's responsible for this mess? It looks like no one. The previous owner can't be held responsible (seller-disclosure laws vary state to state and contain confusing language about responsibilities)), the home inspector can't be held responsible (just check the list of things they can't or won't guarantee), and the government doesn't have any way of holding these inspectors accountable. In fact, most home inspector's contracts have a were n that says something to the effect they the inspector is only liable for a dollar amount equal to the fee charged for the inspection.

So "normal" — for home buyers, and for me — just keeps getting worse. And that's totally unacceptable. I'm out to change that.

I want to see industry standards improve. I want to see more highly skilled, trained inspectors working in the field alongside the few inspectors who already really know their stuff. I've met and worked with some excellent home inspectors — people I wouldn't hesitate to recommend — but even they agree that something has to be done about the inspection industry as a whole. My father was an expert plumber and carpenter, but he knew when to bring in a pro. Likewise, I want to see licensed specialists brought in whenever home inspectors see something that could spell trouble, or whenever they find themselves beyond their own area of expertise.

For all those people who think it's normal to expect a few nasty surprises from a new home, who think that you can't really expect a home inspector to find everything, I'm here to tell you the truth. You should expect quality and integrity in a normal home inspection. You can do better than accept "opinions" in place of evaluations. You can expect a home inspector to give you a thorough assessment of every single part of any home and help you understand what it means.

The cost of an inspection like that may be higher, it's true. But the possible hidden costs of a normal home inspection today — which often isn't worth the paper it's printed on — are far too high already: A bad home inspection can lead to surprises that you will pay for over many years.

My dad is gone now, but I know that he'd be right by my side calling for change and for more integrity in the buying and selling process. Because "normal" — in his book and mine — is just another word for "excellent" or "top-quality" or "as good as it can possibly be." Together, let's demand better home inspections. Let's demand that home inspectors give us more information, better information — all the information that people need to make informed decisions. That's what a normal inspection should be.

— Toronto, 2008

CHAPTER ONE
Why We Need Home Inspections

"What I wish I had known beforehand is how much you cannot trust the home inspector. We almost died from an electrical fire."
— K.T.

"We hired an inspector before we purchased this house, and he pretty much said that everything was fine. He pointed out a few minor electrical things to look into, and when I brought an electrician in, he found many problems in the utility room wiring that my inspector had missed. Later, a plumber came in to install my dishwasher, and the first thing he said was, 'None of this plumbing is up to code.' I know that inspectors aren't supposed to be experts on everything, but it sucks to have tradesmen walk into one room and keep hearing the same thing: 'This isn't right.'"
— R.R.

I hear hundreds of stories just like these — and worse — every week. Can you see why I'm so frustrated? People are getting home inspections done, they're taking advice from "professionals," and they're still buying houses with big unexpected problems.

So many problems that homeowners face — the ones they call in a contractor like me to fix — could be identified even before a house is purchased. The time to find problems is during a home inspection, but, way too often, that's not happening. This is a huge issue for homeowners, who are making the biggest investment of their lives without enough information. You just can't afford to go wrong with that investment.

Here's the good news: when a home inspection is done by a qualified, knowledgeable person before the deal is finalized, and when the buyer really understands what the inspector's report says, buying a house and maintaining it for years to come can be a no-surprises process that works for everyone. In fact, a good home inspection report can become the blueprint for your home maintenance plan.

But after more than two decades of working in this business and seeing too many situations go sour because of unexpected problems — many of which should have been identified by the home inspector — I think it's fair to say that something's not working in this system. It's time for the home inspection industry to give better, more reliable service, and it's time to give homebuyers the information they need to make really informed decisions.

I've written *The Holmes Inspection* to help you make a wise investment. I'm going to show you how to buy with knowledge and not throw your hard-earned dollars into a money pit. I'll show you how to find a reliable home inspector and give you a pretty good idea of what you should be looking out for or asking about when you're checking out a new home to buy. With a thorough home inspection report in your hands, you'll have the negotiating power to buy a house for what it's really worth.

I'm also going to help you sell your house the right way — for a good profit, and with integrity. It might not seem obvious, but a quality home inspection can help you succeed in the selling game as well as in the buying game. When you have your home inspected prior to listing, you get a really good idea of what kind of problems might be going unnoticed. If one home inspector finds those problems, chances are the next one will, too. Once you're aware of the issues, you can choose to fix them or leave them be, knowing that they might become negotiating points for prospective buyers. Either way, you'll be better prepared for selling and better able to present all the facts to potential buyers.

Let's start with a little more detail about home inspections — what a home inspection is, what it should do for you, and the reasons why home inspections aren't always successful. In other words, let's talk about what you really need to know to protect the biggest investment of your life.

What a home inspection is, and what you should get out of it

Home inspectors should provide the reality check that almost every buyer needs. They help you look beyond the surfaces of the house you're considering. They tell you about the condition of the plumbing, the electrical system, the structure, the foundation, the windows, the roof . . . you get the picture. They can tell you the age of the house, and they can spot renovations that have been done — and how well. When they point out problems, they can explain why one problem might be safely overlooked for the time being but why another is serious and will need attention right away. They will show you the relatively cheap fixes and the ones that will cost you a lot of money to make right. That's important information when you're calculating how much you're willing to pay for a house.

Home inspectors should also tell you if they come across something in the house or on the property that they aren't qualified to judge — maybe something structural, or the electrical, plumbing, or HVAC (heating, ventilation, and air conditioning) system. In cases like this, they'll advise you to bring in a licensed specialist.

Just about anybody can see there's something wrong with the ductwork in the left photo. But what about the one on the right? More importantly, are the problems serious, and could they be costly to fix? A home inspector should know — or bring in someone who does.

Luckily for many homebuyers, there are really good home inspectors working in the field who will give you solid information and advice. The best ones are former municipal building inspectors, or people who've worked in the home-building or home-renovation world for years, often in one of the trades or as a general contractor. Unless they were journeymen in one of the trades (such as plumbing, electrical, or carpentry), they're probably generalists rather than specialists. And even though generalists can know a whole lot, they should recognize when they need the help of a specialist.

Good home inspectors are worth their weight in gold, because they'll help you make an informed decision about the house you're investing in. With all the facts at your disposal, you can

- negotiate a fair price for the house based on major deficiencies that it might have at the moment;
- set out a realistic budget for the repairs and upgrades you'll have to do in the future; and
- decide whether you want to buy the house at all or move on to something better.

Why isn't the home inspection process working?

If a process already exists to help people buy with knowledge and confidence, and a lot of people are using that process, why are there still so many stories of houses that disappoint and frustrate their new owners? There are lots of ways to answer that question. Here are my Top 10:

1. INSPECTORS WORK WITHIN SELF-IMPOSED LIMITATIONS.

"Our purchase was on condition of a home inspection, which was completed with no issues. We moved in and discovered that the second-floor heating vents are not connected. We had our home inspector come back, and he said that he doesn't check airflow. He didn't even turn on the furnace."
—K.M.

Most home inspectors' contracts and reports will include a list of things they don't or can't inspect, and it's usually a long one. Generally speaking, home inspectors limit themselves to inspecting what is visible and accessible at the time of the inspection. You might find something like this in the fine print: "The inspector is not permitted to move the personal belongings of the present homeowner. The inspector cannot comment on any conditions that may not have been visually accessible."

The inspector's list of limitations — and just about every home inspection contract contains a list like this — is his protection if you find out that a house you purchased after inspection has serious problems and you try to sue him for your costs.

Many home inspection firms will have you sign a contract before they begin. Part of that contract will specify what the home inspector is not responsible for finding or pointing out to you. Here's a list — compiled from a number of different home inspection contracts — of what your inspector probably won't cover:

- airflow and air quality
- appliances of any kind
- building code compliance
- central vacuum system
- cosmetic items (such as paint)
- environmental risks
- fireplace or wood stove
- intercom
- security and alarm systems
- septic tank system
- spas (including hot tubs, saunas, and steam rooms)
- sprinkler system (in-house)
- swimming pools
- termites or other wood-boring insects, pests, or animal infestation
- toxic substances (mold, fungi, PCBs, lead, asbestos, etc.)
- urea formaldehyde, foam insulation (UFFI)
- perforated pipe bed (presence of pipe, or condition)
- window air conditioner

Woodstoves and fireplaces — either wood-burning or gas — are among the most overlooked features in the home inspection industry. Very few home inspectors are specialists in this area, and some won't look at these features at all.

2. AN INSPECTION IS NOT A WARRANTY.

"We recently purchased our first home, got a home inspection done, and everything sounded great! This spring, as everything melted, we found out the home inspection wasn't as informative as we would have liked. The report stated there was 'evidence of moisture' in the basement walls. The evidence of moisture is now actually streams of water running into the sump well (thank God we have that, at least)."

–A.H.

By law, home inspectors are not responsible for any problems that arise after you buy the house. Their responsibility is limited to what they see on the particular day that they look at a house for you. Often the contract will say that the upper limit of the home inspector's liability is equal to the fee you paid (or something very similar). Even if you won the case, that amount wouldn't cover your legal fees. What you do with the information they pass on is up to you. So when it comes to buying houses, it really is a case of "buyer beware."

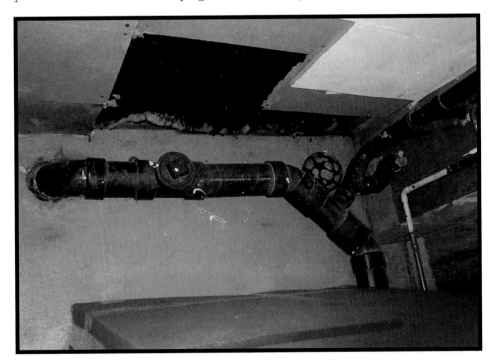

This plumbing is not to code, but it was hidden by the owner's belongings during the inspection. Home inspectors are not permitted to move anything during an inspection, so problems can remain hidden.

3. THERE'S WAY TOO MUCH COOPERATION—EVEN DEPENDENCE— BETWEEN HOME INSPECTORS AND REAL ESTATE AGENTS.

"I had my home inspected by the real estate agent's home inspector because she offers free home inspection when you purchase a home from her. She said she has the best inspector working for her so I went with her choice. Now I realize that there is significant structural damage, and poor contracting work has been done in my home. I feel like I've been taken."
—R.B.

The most common source for a home inspector referral is a real estate agent. The majority of agents are reliable and trustworthy, and it's easy just to call the guy they recommend, but even the most honest agents can't avoid conflict of interest in this particular area. Why not? A real estate agent wants to sell houses. But sometimes an inspector will scare off the buyers if he tells them the whole truth about a house — and that might not make the agent too happy. An inspector wants business. So, to keep the referrals coming from his prime source — the real estate agent — he might not be as thorough as he should be every time he inspects a house. The net result for the homebuyer is not having the whole story before signing a purchase offer.

Keep one thing clear in your dealings with home inspectors: you are the client, and that means you're paying for their objective opinion — the only opinion that's of any use to you. The real estate agent is not the client — at least, she shouldn't be. If the inspector you hire has a history of working with a particular agent, you're walking into a situation of divided loyalties.

Ask your real estate agent for the names and contact information of three home inspectors, and then do your own homework before you decide who to use. (See the checklists on pages 224 and 225.)

4. SOME HOME INSPECTORS DON'T KNOW ENOUGH ABOUT HOUSES OR THE BUILDING TRADES.

"Even though we loved the house, we decided we absolutely must have it inspected given the age (constructed in 1913). We received the all-clear on the inspection, so we went for it. First problem: electrical. A hodge-podge of upgrades and downgrades. The electricians we brought in said they would only do the job if they could do an entire rewiring because it was such a mess. How on earth did this pass inspection?"
—S.H.

I've always said that contractors can be slotted into one of three categories: the good (about 20%), the bad (70%), and the ugly (the remaining 10%).

The "good" are guys with licenses, insurance, skill, experience . . . and integrity. The "bad," who unfortunately account for the majority, aren't trying to take you — they just don't know enough or care enough. The "ugly" are the con artists who just want your money and know how to get it — thankfully, they're in the minority.

I could probably say the same about home inspectors. Too few inspectors are likely to really know their stuff. And I can tell you right now that no one is capable of knowing everything — there's just too much. If someone has worked in the building trades for years and years, there's a good chance that he'll be qualified to work as a home inspector, but even he will need to bring in specialists now and then.

The fact is, way too many inspectors have never worked in the building trades at all.

The jack posts lying on top of old lumber are a sure sign that someone's been tampering with the structure of this house. Was there a building permit? Was the work done right? The inspector who looked at this house didn't notice these posts and didn't ask these crucial questions.

5. INDUSTRY TRAINING AND REGULATION ARE STILL INADEQUATE— ALMOST ANYONE CAN HANG UP A SHINGLE THAT SAYS HE DOES HOME INSPECTIONS.

"We had our home inspected, got the all-clear, and moved in. During our first winter, we found the house to be very cold and damp, so we thought we should have the furnace checked out. The technician determined the furnace to be the type one would use in a mini-home or trailer. Our house is a 4-bedroom split-level. We had to install a new furnace and ducting just to keep my family warm."
–D.L.

There are a couple of issues here. For one thing, the inspection industry in the U.S. is still not standardized or regulated. Some states have licensing and regulations, but others do not. Although national associations of home inspectors are trying to set some standards for training and qualifications, there is no single standard that every home inspector must meet. Second, even if a single industry standard could be agreed on by everyone, would it be a high enough standard to really serve the homebuyers? I go back to my previous point: too many home inspectors just don't know enough about the building trades to give reliable advice.

6. SELLERS DON'T ALWAYS DISCLOSE WHAT THEY SHOULD.

"Problems started the day the deal closed: the basement sewer backed up. The cause turned out to be extensive root penetration in the old clay drains. The sellers claimed they didn't know of any root problems but further investigation found they had applied for a grant from the city for that very thing. Estimates for repair are in excess of $12,000."
–K.J.

The financial stakes are high when it comes to buying and selling houses, and some sellers can't resist the temptation to stretch the truth about their home's merits. They may also withhold the truth about their home's problems.

In more that half of the states in the U.S., sellers are asked to fill out a disclosure form that lists known problems or conditions in the house. Depending on where you live, it might be called a property condition disclosure statement or a seller property information statement. But there is not currently a national disclosure form.. Depending on the state, the seller answers questions about a whole range of issues, including ownership, zoning, current or pending historical designation, possible environmental contamination, and structural matters.

The form is supposed to be filled out accurately, but sellers are on their honor. Sellers' liabilities are limited, and the forms can be vague about known vs. unknown conditions. And real estate agents' contracts also limit their liability, saying that responsibility to disclose rests with the seller.

What all this means is that the onus is on the buyer to make sure that the disclosure form is telling the whole truth. Sometimes new owners will discover a major defect in their house and then try to sue the previous owner for not disclosing the problem. Suing — or being sued — can cost you a lot of money in legal fees, and the outcome is never guaranteed. Because the whole process of disclosure is so filled with pitfalls, if it's not required by a particular state, some lawyers recommend not filling out the form at all when it's time for you to sell your place.

On the flip side, as a buyer, don't trust disclosure forms. Make sure for yourself that the house you're buying is a good bet and worth the money.

Real "fluffing" when you're selling

Forget the fresh-baked bread at the open house. Have an inspection report ready plus complete documentation of all work done to the house, including permits, warranties, and photographs. And be sure to have your utility bills available so buyers can assess the heating and air-conditioning costs.

This will really impress buyers, and it will give them informa-tion they can actually use. Documentation like this should be the standard — not the exception — for every home on the market.

7. THE RISE OF "FLUFFING AND FLIPPING"—IT'S JUST LIPSTICK AND MASCARA.

"The house looked great, but later we discovered that the previous owners had done cosmetic 'upgrades' in the cheapest way possible, probably just to sell the home. Let's just say it's obvious that we were novice buyers."
–C.G.

We're all now familiar with television shows (and magazine articles and books) that tell people how to "fluff" their house before putting it on the market. You know the kind of advice they give: get rid of the clutter, paint in neutral colors, do some cosmetic upgrades, have some bread baking in the oven during the open house. There's nothing wrong with putting your best foot forward to get a good price for your house, but sometimes the underlying message of this growing new industry is that it's okay to knowingly distract prospective buyers from a home's serious defects, or even to cover up those defects.

8. HOME INSPECTION CHECKLISTS USUALLY DON'T TELL THE WHOLE STORY, AND SOME INSPECTORS DON'T COMMUNICATE WELL ENOUGH TO LET YOU KNOW WHEN THERE IS A SERIOUS PROBLEM.

"We are having the windows replaced this week because the existing ones were sieves that created three climate zones in winter, one being 'outside mode.' I want to choke the home inspector — I asked him three times about the windows because my gut told me they needed to be replaced."
—M.R.

If you've been through at least one home inspection in your lifetime, you'll know what I'm talking about: the reports are based on checklists, with lots of little boxes and comment choices like "adequate" or "generally acceptable" or "needs improvement."

Yes, it's a report card for a house. Just as your report cards likely didn't tell the whole story about how you were doing at school, an inspector's report sometimes hides more than it reveals. And if the inspector you've hired isn't that good at communicating, that's another obstacle, because you might need someone to say to you, "This home is a safety hazard. Do not buy this house." You don't want a message like that buried in a checklist.

9. A HOME INSPECTION AS A CONDITION OF AN OFFER IS SOMETIMES TOO LITTLE INFORMATION, TOO LATE.

"We were in the process of buying a house and brought in a home inspector. Within the first 15 minutes, the inspector discovered he could push the exterior stucco walls inward with his hands. Not a good sign. He said, 'I wouldn't buy this house based on the stucco job and I haven't even been inside.' He completed the inspection, since we had already paid him, and found even more appalling things — countertops not secured, exhaust fans that vented into the garage instead of outside, a laundry room on the second floor that wasn't big enough for any machines, and no drainage. The inspector's $300 fee paid off in less than 15 minutes."
–K.C.

A home inspection should always be part of the home-buying process, and buyers need to take this step seriously. An inspection is not useful if it is done too late. Sometimes people will hire an inspector before making an offer, but all too frequently buyers don't start looking for an inspector until the offer has already been made. This gives them less time to find the right inspector, and they may end up hiring the only one that's available.

To complicate the matter, by the time most buyers make an offer, they are already pretty much sold on the place, and it would take a serious warning to turn them off the house. Home inspectors don't want to influence clients too much, so they often don't give them serious warnings. They hedge, saying things like "may be a problem," "improve or rectify," or "will need attention." Getting the inspection done before any offer has been made will help buyers remain objective about the house.

Sometimes buyers include a home inspection as a condition of the offer, treating the inspection mainly as a stalling tactic to firm up financing. Buyers who do this clearly don't take the inspection seriously and won't pay enough attention to the process.

So think about the home inspection before you make your offer. You may end up paying for the inspection of a house you're not going to buy, but it's worth every penny if it saves you from high stress and potential financial disaster.

10. SOME HOMEBUYERS THINK A HOME INSPECTION IS JUST A HOOP THEY HAVE TO JUMP THROUGH.

"The inspector didn't want us to go with him on the day of the inspection. We didn't like the idea, but we had no choice, and what harm would it be, anyway? A few hours later we got our report, which said the place was in excellent/good shape. We were shocked by the problems that started showing when we moved in, and there's been nothing but trouble ever since."
—L.M.

Some homebuyers don't even show up for the home inspection they're paying for. That's a mistake. Some people go through the inspection, but they don't take it too seriously or don't think too much about what the inspector has to say.

Here's the bottom line when you're buying: You absolutely have to be there when the home inspection is taking place. You have to listen to what you're hearing, and ask questions to make sure you understand. You need to understand the implications of what the inspector is telling you, or you will not be buying with your eyes open.

You don't need to be an expert at everything; just at what you get paid to do in life. But when the time comes to buy a home, educate yourself as much as you can. Use the home inspector's expertise — however much he has — as much as you can. Remember: the home inspector is going to get paid the same amount no matter what he tells you or doesn't tell you. But if you aren't paying attention and asking questions — or if you aren't even there — you might be the one who pays too much for a money pit of a house.

The railing in this house passed the home inspection. The railing's improper height and poor-quality materials are red flags.

I know, I know: all this sounds scary.

"Forget a home inspector," you're thinking. "I don't even want to buy a house."

But I'm here to tell you that buying a house is still one of the most rewarding things you can do — for your financial portfolio, for your lifestyle, and for your family. And it can be done with minimal risk — if you get the facts and if you demand the best from the people who are there to advise you. Quality home inspections are an important part of minimizing the risk.

I also want you to know that this book, even though it contains a lot of information that you need to know when you're buying or selling, is not a substitute for a home inspection. I believe that home inspections — the right kind, done by the most qualified people, using the best technology available today, and supplemented by other experts in the residential housing field — can and should be an essential part of the home-buying and home-selling process. And keep in mind that a thorough home inspection report can be very useful after you buy a home. You can use the inspection report as an accurate road map of what needs doing when maintaining your new home or thinking about a renovation.

And you shouldn't worry if you get a home inspection and it shows some problems. There's no such thing as the perfect house. In fact, if the home inspector doesn't find something wrong with the house, the inspection probably hasn't been done right.

At the moment, the home inspection industry needs improvement. It needs higher standards, better training, and more rigorous requirements for the people who use the title "home inspector." All that may be on its way. I sure hope it is, and I'm doing what I can to help make it happen.

But no matter how much the industry improves, one thing will continue to be true: average people need to be informed about how to buy, how to sell, and how their homes really work. If you want to own a house, you have to know something about how it works. There really is no way to avoid this. You don't have to know how to build a house or how to renovate it, or even how to hang a picture on the wall, but you have to know enough to judge whether you're getting a good deal or getting shafted. Just compare the process of buying a house to buying a car: You'd do research on the best models, the best years, maybe find out what other car owners had to say. You'd look under the hood, you'd go for a test drive, find out about mileage. And you'd get a safety check, that's for sure. You'd really look into the vehicle.

How much bigger an investment is a house? Educating yourself is worth it.

First things first. Let's look at how to find and hire the right people when you're buying or selling a home. You can make it right — even before you sign on the dotted line.

CHAPTER TWO
Slow Down—
Then Hire Right

"Only needs cosmetic work," I was told by the home inspector. I moved in and found the electrical and plumbing both in need of a complete overhaul. The worst thing I could have done was to hire a home inspector who was friends with the seller's real estate agent. How could I not have known better?
—C.I.

"When we bought our house a few months ago, we didn't hire a home inspector because the bank said they were going to send an inspector to see if the house was worth the money before approving the financing. We didn't realize it was just a drive-by. We got the house, and now we've found out that we need a whole new roof."
—P.M.

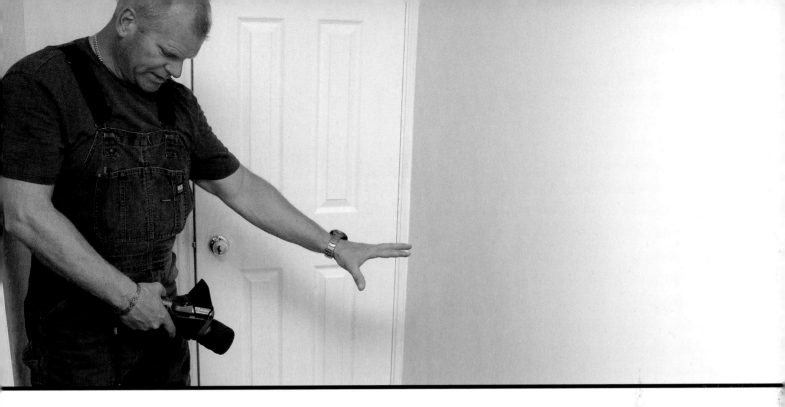

Hiring the first inspector you call is like playing the slot machines — your chance of turning up a winner is just that — chance.

We live in an instant-gratification, "on demand" world. If we want something — from fast-food to furniture to a new car — we go get it. In my first book, *Make It Right*, I warned against taking that approach to home renovations. Many horror stories of renovations gone wrong can be avoided, I wrote, if you slow down, educate yourself about the process, and hire the right people.

The same is true of buying or selling that house. It takes time to do it right.

Sometimes people are forced by circumstance to buy or sell their home quickly. They get a new job in a different city, they get transferred, or a change in their personal life makes it necessary for them to act quickly. But in many cases, probably the majority, people get caught up in the emotional excitement of buying a home, and they move way too fast — even when there's no rush at all.

Take your time and make sure you really know what you're getting, because you're probably going to be stuck with that house for a long time. Slow down, educate yourself about the process, and hire the right people.

First, let's discuss real estate agents, and how you should find and choose the one who's going to do the job right for you.

When you're buying, your agent is your first line of defense against buying a defective house. An agent who is really working for you (not just trying to get a quick sale) should make you aware of possible problems with any house you look at, pointing out things to ask the home inspector about.

When you're selling, a realtor can suggest the most important improvements to make to get the best price, such as painting or fixing various things around the house. But this is also where a home inspection is extremely valuable — get one done before you list your house for sale. While the agent will be more aware of how things look, the home inspector will focus on mechanical and structural issues. Consult both, and you'll have a complete to-do list.

HIRING RIGHT: REAL ESTATE AGENTS

What you want in a real estate agent will vary slightly depending on whether you're buying or selling a house, but the basic qualities you'll need are the same: experience, market savvy, negotiating skills, dedication to the job, flexibility, honesty — and undivided loyalty. In the U.S., it's traditional and more common for a real estate agent to list a house for sale for the seller. Both would sign a contract, and when the house sold, the agent would be paid a percentage of the sale price. If you go with that same agent to look at houses to buy, the agent is actually working for the seller of the house. Or, if you find an agent you like, you can sign a buyer's contract, which means the agent is working for you, the buyer. Buyer's contracts have gotten more popular in the last 15 years. When you buy a house, you still don't have to pay the agent with whom you have a buyer's contract; his/her fee is paid by the seller as a percentage of the sale price.

It's possible that your agent could end up working for both you and the other party. This is called dual agency, and it's not unethical as long as the agent makes sure you know about it. And you should make sure to ask.

For a start, you can find names of agents by looking at the signs around town. Take note of the people whose names seem to appear again and again on "for sale" signs, especially on homes that seem to sell quickly. This is especially important if you're looking to sell your house — you want someone who's good at selling. To be more methodical about the process, you can call different real estate agencies and ask who their top sellers are. Be aware that if you go into a real estate office, you will likely find yourself talking with an agent immediately. They won't want you to get away, but don't be pressured into signing an agreement with anybody until you've had a chance to do your homework to determine who you really want to work with.

Another way to find an agent is through referrals. No doubt you know other people who've bought and sold houses in your area, and they can probably recommend someone to you. But don't just take their word that the agent is good — ask lots of questions about their experiences working with that person.

Start with the basics, like finding out if the agent helped them with buying or selling, or both. Was it one house or more than one? How long did the buying/selling process take? Was the agent good at explaining the process to them? Was he or she knowledgeable about the real estate market? If it was a buying situation, was the agent willing to show them lots of places without complaints or pressure tactics? A good agent understands that the "soft sell" is better than the quick one. They'd rather show you lots of houses and find the right one than have you put your money down on the first one you see. They know they'll get repeat business from you in the future, and from other people you'll refer, if they put your needs first.

Did the agent point out flaws in the houses the buyers looked at, so they'd be well informed about what they were seeing, or did he or she try to convince them that every house they looked at was exactly what they were looking for? And did the agent respect the client's budget?

The answers to these questions can help you weed out some names and put others on a list of possibles. But don't make a final decision until you've interviewed a number of people and found the right fit.

Finding the right agent is absolutely critical to buying right. I always like to hear about agents who aren't afraid to say, "Forget this house. It's too much money. You can do better." That tells me you're working with someone who'd rather sell you the right house than just any house.

MIKE'S TIPS

Here are the most important questions to ask a real estate agent:

How long have you been working as a real estate agent?

How many buyers have you successfully represented in the past six months? Can I have the names and phone numbers of three to six of your most recent clients? (Following up on these references is critical.)

How will you protect my interests, and why should I hire you rather than another agent?

5 questions to ask your real estate agent about any house you're considering

Once you start looking at houses, lots of questions will occur to you. Many will be specific to your own needs and to the particular houses you're looking at, but here are a few that you should keep in mind and ask every time.

1. HOW OLD IS THE HOUSE?
More than anything else, the age of the house will tell you what to expect. The rule is pretty predictable: the older the house, the more likely it will need major repairs and reno. But don't assume that all newer homes are problem-free. When a house (or a renovation) gets to be 20 or 30 years old, lots of things start breaking down. But some new homes are not so much built as slammed together and can hide all kinds of problems just waiting to appear.

2. HOW LONG HAS THE SELLER OWNED THE HOUSE?
This is a really important question. Very brief ownership (anything less than a year), and you might be looking at a "flip." That's when someone buys a house, fixes it up, and then resells, looking for a quick profit. There are good and bad flips, but far too often a flip is the worst kind of "lipstick and mascara" job, where they've made a lot of cosmetic changes and overlooked (or covered up) the mechanical and structural issues.

3. WHAT'S THE SALES AND RENOVATION HISTORY OF THIS HOUSE?
Your agent will be able to produce for you a list of recent sales activity on the house you're looking at. You'll want this for a couple of reasons: For one thing, it will tell you if the house has been bought and sold a lot. Lots of sales activity might be a sign of big problems with the house — as each new buyer discovers he's been taken for a ride, he decides to get off that merry-go-round by selling the house and all its headaches to someone else. On the more positive side, a list of recent sales can help you determine if the asking price is fair. You'll be able to see how much the previous owner paid for the house and when, and your agent can find out (from the vendor's agent) what changes or improvements have been made since that time. Fair market value is not simple arithmetic, though: it also takes into account the natural rise in land and housing prices, especially in hot real estate markets.

4. ARE THERE BUILDING PERMITS OR INSPECTION REPORTS FOR ANY WORK DONE ON THIS HOUSE?

Most renovations require building permits from your local building authority. City Hall is a good starting point for locating them. In some towns and cities, you can now search electronically by street address for a home's permit history. Those permits, along with the inspection reports that are made at various stages of the work, are important records of what's been done. It's ideal if the seller has kept the permits and makes them available to prospective buyers. For structural, plumbing, and electrical work, it's safest if you have hard evidence that the work was inspected and approved by building authorities.

5. WAS THIS HOUSE EVER USED TO MANUFACTURE NARCOTICS?

Believe it or not, there are many houses that have been used to manufacture and grow drugs. Not all states require this information to be disclosed to potential buyers, but more and more states are making it a requirement. In Texas and California, for instance, it's required as part of a disclosure statement to say whether a building was ever used to manufacture methamphetamines, which leave behind myriad toxic waste. And the high humidity levels needed to grow marijuana indoors can lead to lots of mold problems in a building. Drug manufacturing usually involves some dangerous "retrofitting" of the structure and electrical systems. There may be outstanding remedies ordered by the local building authority. Ask any real estate agent you are considering about the laws in your state and whether he or she has ever had to deal with former drug houses. An experienced realtor might even be able to spot the telltale signs.

Serious mould problems are usually present in a house that has been a marijuana-grow operation.

HIRING RIGHT: HOME INSPECTORS

Once you've jumped into the pool of potential houses on the market, it probably won't be long before you find one that you're getting serious about. For some people, that's when they make their first call to a home inspector. I think that's leaving it way too late.

The best time to look for a home inspector is at the same time or even before you look for an agent. As I've always said about finding the best contractors, don't underestimate how long this part of the process will take, and don't take shortcuts — it's too important. When you think about the fact that whoever you hire is going to advise you on a purchase that you'll be paying for over the next 25 years, week after week, month after month, it makes sense to slow down and hire right.

And if you wait to find a home inspector until you're already in a high-pressure competitive bidding situation, the odds are you'll break down and do one of three things:

One, you'll decide to go it alone and forget about the home inspection. Not a good idea. Are you really prepared to invest that much money in an emotional response?

Two, you'll hire the first inspector you call. Just as I've said many times about hiring contractors, if you don't do your homework before you hire, you might as well try your luck at the slot machines.

Three, you'll hire the inspector your agent recommends. As I said in the previous chapter, I don't recommend using a home inspector just because your agent recommends him. There's a conflict of interest, and I think it's best to do independent research to find an inspector who will give you unbiased advice. You might end up hiring the very guy your agent would recommend, but you need to determine for yourself that you've found the right person for the job.

The process of finding an inspector is much like the process I've recommended for finding a real estate agent or, in my previous book, finding a contractor. You start with a list of names — whether from public sources, such as online directories or the Yellow Pages, or from friends and acquaintances — and then you contact those people and ask questions until you've got the answers you need.

One of the first things you'll notice about home inspectors is that most of them will list a lot of initials after their name. The initials tell you what professional associations the inspector belongs to, and this is supposed to give you peace of mind about hiring him. These guys are accredited or licensed, so they must be well trained, right?

Well, not necessarily.

MIKE'S TIPS
The most important questions to ask when you're hiring a home inspector

How long have you been in business as a home inspector?

Did you have any experience in the building trades before becoming a home inspector? If so, what kind, and for how long? (Look for people who've worked in the building trades as electricians, plumbers, carpenters, general contractors, engineers, municipal building inspectors, etc.)

Do you belong to an association of home inspectors? Are you a certified member? Can you provide me with at least 10 references for people who have hired you in the past three to five years? (Following up on these references is critical. You need to ask people what kind of experience they had with this inspector, whether they were surprised by any problems that cropped up after they bought their homes, and whether they would hire the inspector again in the future.)

It is true that national home inspection associations exist, and almost every decent home inspector will belong to one of them. Each of these associations has its own set of standards. Usually they have membership categories based on the individual members' qualifications and experience, and members cannot advertise or promote their membership in the association until they have reached certain minimum standards. Becoming a member involves taking courses, passing tests, and, often, conducting a certain number of inspections that meet the association's standards.

Again, you have to ask questions: How high are the standards? How good are those courses? Can the skills that a home inspector needs be taught in a six-week course? That's right: to achieve minimum accreditation in most of these associations, all that's required is a six-week course. Some franchises provide their franchisees with only two weeks of training (not all of it on home inspecting itself) before giving them a "home inspection certificate." If I'm going to spend the next 25 years or so paying off a house, I'd like to know that the person who advised me on its quality had more than six weeks (or two) of training.

When you're hiring a home inspector, there are some things you might hear that should jump out as big red warning flags. I'd steer clear of anyone who says or does the following:

- You ask a prospective home inspector about his qualifications and he doesn't have much of an answer for you. Real pros — of any kind — love to tell you about the work they've done. He should offer you a lot of information about himself, his certification, the association he belongs to, and his company.
- You call to arrange a home inspection and are told that the inspector can only find time to do it at night. No home inspection should ever be done without adequate daylight — it's just not possible to spot exterior problems without enough light. The guy who conducts home inspections at night is not a true professional.
- The inspector tells you there's a certain problem with the house you want to buy — then tells you he can fix it for you after the house is yours. Under their professional code of ethics as set out by the various associations, home inspectors shouldn't offer any repair, renovation, or improvement services. Nor should they be associated with any other construction or house-related trade — even though some franchises do attempt to do both.

A home inspector is an inspector—period. He should not offer contracting or renovating services as well. It's a clear conflict of interest.

MIKE'S TIPS
Building inspectors, home inspectors: What's the difference?

Don't be confused by terminology: there are home inspectors and there are building inspectors, and they are two very different occupations.

Building inspectors are employees of municipal governments. They're the people who inspect your home as it's being built or renovated, to ensure that the work meets the local minimum building code. The process is set into motion when you or your contractor takes out a building permit for a specific job. Beyond the cost of the permit, you don't pay for the services of a building inspector.

Building inspectors often have different specializations: one might inspect structural things (foundations, walls, doors, windows) while another person is responsible for plumbing inspections and another for electrical. Usually these inspectors will check out a job at very specific stages in the process. It's the law to do it this way, and a good contractor cooperates willingly.

Home inspectors are in private business. (They are also referred to as "home and property inspectors," with property inspectors specializing in commercial buildings.) They may work independently, for a small firm, or for one of the nationwide home inspection companies. You pay for their services on either a flat-rate or an hourly basis.

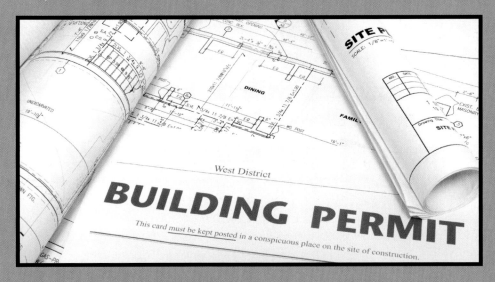

WHAT YOU CAN EXPECT TO PAY

The cost of an inspection depends on three things: the size of the house and lot; the city or area you live in (inspectors in urban centers may charge more); and, most important, the complexity of the house and the range of services offered by the inspector (some inspectors specialize in identifying mold and other contaminants, but these services are extra). According to the U.S. Department of Housing and Urban Development (HUD) the inspection of a home will cost $300-$500.

For what you're getting, that price may be reasonable, and if the home inspector is really good at his job, $500 is a bargain. On the other hand, if the home inspector doesn't find and point out major flaws in the house before you buy, you've paid too much for his "opinion."

The very best home inspections do not come cheap. And they shouldn't. Think about it: we're talking about your home, your biggest investment. The more wisely you spend your money in the beginning, the more you'll save in the long run.

Complete, thorough home inspections should cost anywhere from $350 to $500 right up to $2,000 (if you bring in other professionals), depending on the size and complexity of the house. For that price you can expect to get professional evaluations from licensed contractors, rather than the opinion of a single person who may or may not have experience in the most important areas of home building (electrical, plumbing, structure, and HVAC), and maybe some others too (fireplace specialists, gas specialists, toxic mold specialists, and so on).

Right now very few home inspection companies can offer that range of professional services or will bring in those licensed professionals to give you a complete evaluation.

WHEN YOU NEED TO CALL IN OTHER PROFESSIONALS

Ideally, every home inspection would involve licensed professionals from the major trades: electrical, plumbing, structure, and HVAC. But there are times when bringing in these professionals is more important than others.

In older homes where nothing, or almost nothing, has been done to the house, it's likely that a good home inspector can tell you what you're seeing. Depending on the age of the house, there will be some degree of deterioration, and certain parts will probably be nearing the end of their useful life, but at least it should be obvious how well the house was built.

When you find a house that makes big promises, however, that's when you need to get more advice. For me, the red flag goes up when I see "completely renovated" or "like new." This usually means an older home with a lot of renovations done to it, and when that happens there are plenty of opportunities for things to have been done wrong. Plumbing, for instance: does the new plumbing tie in properly to the old? With a finished basement, is there a proper thermal break between the basement walls and the finished drywall? What about a thermal break between the concrete basement floor and whatever has been laid down as a finish flooring? These are situations when a licensed plumber and a licensed carpenter need to be brought in to advise you. You can expect to pay at least $55 per hour for a licensed contractor's time, maybe more if it's just a one-shot deal rather than part of a bigger job.

It's easy to spot the "curb appeal" differences in these photos, but only a close inspection will reveal all the real issues. Look carefully at so-called "like new" properties.

1. The word "condominium" refers to a legal structure of shared ownership, not to a physical structure. That means a condominium corporation can be set up almost anywhere, in any type of building — apartment-style, townhouses, detached homes converted into several units, resort properties, etc.

2. When you buy a condominium unit, you're purchasing everything you can see within the four walls of your unit, plus a portion of the "common elements" — that's the legal term for everything that's shared, including the roof, driveway, hallways, and features like swimming pools and exercise rooms. Each owner pays a monthly condo fee to the condominium corporation for the upkeep of these common elements.

3. You can pay for different types of condominium inspections. The first is a basic inspection of the interior elements of the unit, including the floors, walls, windows, kitchen and bathrooms, and whatever can be seen of the plumbing, electrical, and heating. I recommend the second type of inspection, which involves the unit as well as the rest of the condominium development. Even this can be limited, because the inspector usually can't get access to the entire building and because the building might be too large to inspect thoroughly.

4. The windows, plumbing, electrical, and heating of most condominium buildings are considered common elements. That means any costs for repairs or upgrades to these will be covered by the condominium corporation on an ongoing basis — using the monthly condo fees that each owner pays. But if you want to renovate your kitchen, for example, you'll pay for any changes made to the plumbing or electrical.

5. You probably won't be able to change any elements (such as windows) that affect the exterior appearance of the building, since most condo corporations like to keep a uniform look on the outside. Check out the limitations before you buy.

6. Condo corporations are required by law to keep a reserve fund for capital expenses. If the roof needs to be reshingled or the driveway needs to be repaved, the reserve fund will cover those costs. A percentage of your condo fees is paid into this reserve fund every month. But — this is really important to know — if a major expense comes up unexpectedly and the reserve fund isn't big enough to pay for it, the corporation will make a "special assessment," and you'll be required to pay your portion of this extra cost.

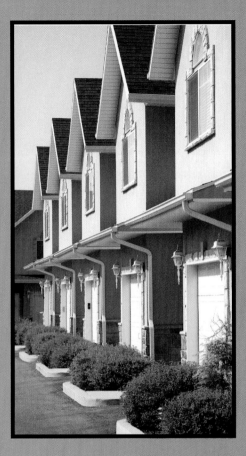

7. Prior to buying a condo, you need to do your homework. Request from the condo corporation at least the previous two years of minutes from its monthly meetings. From these, you'll find out about any issues in the development, and you'll see whether there are plans being made for big expenses in the near future. Review this information carefully — it could tell you whether you want to invest or walk away. Get legal advice if you don't understand everything that's there.

8. Buying new? Get an inspection. A home inspector will help you come up with an itemized list of what's unfinished or needs to be touched up before you move in — it becomes your "to-do" list for the builder. Once you've got that list, follow up on it with the builder, and don't sign those final papers until you're satisfied that everything's been done.

9. Second piece of advice when you're buying new: consult an experienced real estate lawyer to help you determine if the corporation's plan for the future (and the reserve fund) make the development a safe investment.

10. Condominium ownership can be great for people who don't want the hassle of maintaining a house. It's also good for people who travel a lot and don't want to worry about an empty house, for those with less mobility, or for those who just don't want to shovel their own snow. But keep in mind that there is no way to avoid the cost of maintaining a home, even when the costs are shared among many owners. That monthly fee will always be there, and you'd better hope that your condo corporation is made up of people who really know how to manage and maintain the property.

A REALITY CHECK ABOUT HOUSES AND HOME-BUYING

No matter who you hire to inspect your house before you buy, you're going to discover something really important: absolutely every house will need some work, especially over time. That may sound totally obvious, but to some people it's not. At the beginning of this chapter I said that we live in an instant-gratification, "on demand" world. I could easily add "maintenance-free" to that description, which explains why I actually have to state that all houses require maintenance. Everybody wants to buy something that's in perfect shape and will always stay that way. But nothing is truly maintenance-free. Not your truck, your tools, your relationships — and for sure not your house.

Because most people don't have enough knowledge about how houses work and because they aren't realistic about what it takes to care for a house, they buy a home in the worst possible way: they judge solely on appearances and they buy based on emotions.

Knowing that a house needs work shouldn't discourage you. And it shouldn't keep you from buying. What's important is to know how much you'll have to put into the house in order to bring it up to your standards (or keep it there), and whether you can afford that. Most home inspection reports will have a statement like this about the normal costs of maintaining a house: "The inspection and report are not intended to identify minor and usual cosmetic repairs or maintenance items. A second-hand property normally requires 3% of the total property value in repairs, replacements, and maintenance in the first year of ownership." Some will also state that an owner should expect to pay 3% to 5% as the yearly cost of maintenance. I believe the amount depends on the quality of the house when you buy and the standards you want to maintain. You could spend more than that figure, or less.

Before you head out into the housing market, keep in mind that the power really is in your hands. You have the power to hire the best realtor and the best home inspector. With your eyes open and realistic plans in place, you have the potential to buy a great home.

And though it's easy to feel intimidated by the process, just keep this in mind: you're the one who's footing the bill for all these services. It's your right to get the best service and the most comprehensive information. Demand it, and don't apologize for being demanding.

CHAPTER THREE
The Exterior

"We have spent about $75,000 renovating our home, with little money left to fix the outside because we were assured by the home inspector that everything was in good condition outside. If we'd known it was in such bad shape, we would have done less work inside and saved a good chunk of money to fix outside."
—A.F.

The inspection of any house starts with the big picture.

By the time you call your home inspector to look at a house, you've probably been through that house at least once already. You know you're serious about it, and maybe you've even got an offer in. More than likely there's something about the house that impresses you, some fancy details that you really like — maybe granite counters in the kitchen, or a hot tub on the back deck. Maybe it just satisfies some basic needs — it's close to your work or the expressway, or it has the right number of bedrooms.

Whatever has taken you this far along, you want to put your emotions and assumptions aside. It's important to feel good about the house you're going to buy, but it's even more important to have solid facts about it. Now is the time to step back and look at it objectively.

A home inspection is more than just a formality. You are here to determine if this house is a good enough, safe enough place to invest your money. From beginning to end, you want to look at this house as if it's your first time through. Start with the big picture, but also take note of the smallest details. Don't make up your mind until you've seen — really seen — everything.

BEFORE YOU GO

When you go along on a home inspection, you're not the one doing the inspection. The inspector you've hired will do the inspection, and your job is to get as much information as you can so that you can make an educated decision about the house.

I recommend that you bring the following things with you for every inspection:

- this book, to consult checklists from the appendix and make notes
- a measuring tape
- a flashlight
- binoculars, for a better view of the chimney and roof
- a camera
- tissues, to check for drafts around doors and windows and to check exhaust fans

THE SITE

One of the keys to the success or failure of any house has to do with just one thing: how it handles water. Water comes in many forms — rain, snow, condensation, and even the water table (ground water) underneath the house. We also bring water into our homes through our plumbing systems and get rid of it through drainage and waste systems. Water is a necessity of life, but it also has the potential to cause rot and mould, endanger human health, and destroy entire buildings.

When we stand back and look at a house, the site is the first indication of whether there will be water problems inside the house. Take a look at how high the house sits in relation to the land: Is it built on or near the top of a hill? In a valley or on a slope? Is it on completely flat ground?

Ideally, you're looking for a place on fairly high ground, because water will naturally drain away from high places — and away from your house. If the house is in a low-lying area, it's almost certain to have more water issues to deal with. (Being on the top of a hill is not ideal either, since it can be windy and expensive to heat.)

To assess the potential for water problems, look at the relationship between the foundation and the land right next to it. In the best-case scenario, there will be a slight downward slope to the land as you move away from the house. In other words, the highest point will be right next to the foundation, with the land gently sloping away from it. You need a slope of at least five degrees to keep all water moving away from the foundation rather than toward it. You can determine the degree of slope by taking a simple measurement: for every foot away from the foundation wall, the ground should drop by a ½ inch; over a 6-foot span, that will amount to a difference of 3 inches.

Sometimes just one or two places around the house will cause drainage problems. For instance, maybe there's a walkway or paved driveway along one side, and over time the pavement has heaved in such a way that it's now sloping towards the house: this is going to increase the amount of water that your foundation has to repel.

Window wells around basement windows should be filled with gravel, and you should see the end of a length of some drainage tile (also filled with gravel). If everything's been done right, that drainage tile will lead to the foundation drain, keeping water away from your foundation.

Another common culprit is the garden. Flower beds with a high mound of soil that drops off at the front and back can cause rainwater to flow back against the house. Watering plants so close to the house is also dangerous for foundations. The best plants to have next to the foundation are ones that don't require additional watering (apart from rainfall).

This window well (left) looks good, with corrugated plastic drainage tile. It's impossible to know if the tile is properly connected to the perforated pipeat the base of the house (most municipalities don't allow storm connection), but if there is a problem, there might be signs of water damage in the basement.

Overgrown greenery (below left) could be preventing proper drainage around this foundation. A splash block (below right) keeps water away from the foundation, but this downspout is still too close to the house.

Downspouts (the vertical pipes that are connected to the gutters) can cause water problems in the basement if they are inadequate or broken. Is there a downspout for each length of gutter? Are they properly connected to the gutters? Do they extend at least several feet from the house and deposit the water on soil that slopes away from the house? They should empty onto a splash block or collect in a rain barrel or some other type of reservoir.

RED FLAGS FOR THE SITE
- house sits too low or too high in relation to surrounding land
- window wells with inadequate drainage
- landscaping that causes rainwater to flow back against foundation, or that requires heavy watering
- downspouts are damaged or missing, or they discharge too close to the foundation
- depressions in the soil or standing water around foundation. Drainage is an issue, and the basement should be examined carefully for signs of moisture problems.

THE YARD

Most people would agree that a yard should look well cared for, especially when the house is on the market. Mature trees are usually considered a selling feature. Beyond that, the pros and cons of any yard are mostly a matter of individual preference.

Ask yourself if the yard, as it currently stands, will meet your needs, or if it can be modified.

Drainage shouldn't be a problem for a house that's sited on such high ground. That retaining wall around the stairs and sidewalk, however, will need special attention over the years.

RED FLAGS FOR THE YARD
- not enough room for gardening, for young children to play, etc.
- not fenced for privacy and safety, or fence is in need of repair
- lawn and/or garden requiring too much maintenance
- no mature trees or other landscaping features
- mature trees that create too much shade indoors
- mature trees planted too close to house. Overhanging branches can damage shingles, gutters, and downspouts. Root systems can interfere with plumbing, the waste line to the municipal sewers or septic system, and even the foundation.

THE DRIVEWAY

In most cities there are just a few driveway options: unpaved, or paved with asphalt, concrete, or interlocking bricks. It's considered a selling point to have a paved driveway — of any kind — because snow removal is so difficult on gravel driveways. The lifespan of a paved driveway will depend on the quality and thickness of the materials used, how well the surface underneath was prepared (a thick enough layer of gravel and proper tamping), and how often and well it's been maintained.

Ask the homeowner how old the driveway surface is, and ask about any maintenance that's been done. Look for signs of age, wear, and damage.

 RED FLAGS FOR DRIVEWAYS
- loose, broken, or cracked bricks
- depressions, cracks, or holes in asphalt
- faded and tired-looking asphalt
- hairline cracks or major cracks in concrete
- an incorrect slope that will draw water toward the house or garage rather than toward the street and storm sewers

Someone has taken a stab at sealing the gap where brick and driveway meet. The crevices and cracks — not to mention sloppiness — are signs of what an inadequate job this is.

THE ROOF AND RELATED SYSTEMS: FIRST DEFENSE AGAINST THE ELEMENTS

If the success of any house depends, as I said before, on how well it defends itself (and the people in it) against water, then the roof is the first of several make-or-break components. Whether a roof is peaked or flat, its job is to shed water, protecting the top of the house and keeping as much water as possible from even touching other parts of the house, through the use of overhangs and gutters.

When you start looking at houses, you'll want to know some basics about how they work and how they wear over time. For starters, you should know about the pitch of a roof. Pitch is usually described as a ratio between the vertical and horizontal dimensions, which are called the rise and the run. You might hear someone say that a roof is "2 in 12," which means that for every 2 feet of rise, there are 12 feet of run. That's a fairly low pitch — in fact, anything less is considered a flat roof and has to be treated completely differently from a conventional sloped roof. A fairly common slope or pitch is 4 (or higher) in 12.

There are pros and cons to every type of roof, but in general a roof with a steep pitch will have a longer lifespan. This is because steep roofs repel water and snow better than flatter roofs do, and therefore they aren't damaged as much by the elements.

No matter what type of roofing material you use, its worst enemy is the sun. Over time, sunlight will wear out almost any type of shingle or roof covering — you can see this by looking at the difference in the amount of wear on the south and west sides of a roof in comparison to the east and north sides.

Low-sloped roofs often have problems with ice accumulating on the lower edges. Inadequate insulation can be the cause, but it's usually difficult to insulate and ventilate roofs that are low-sloped, because there just isn't much room for either insulation or air movement. This means that ice-dam problems can be chronic.

It's also good to know that some of the best-looking roofs can be the most difficult to look after. Dormers and gables, for instance, are great details, but because they create a lot of intersecting planes on the rooftop, they have the potential to cause moisture problems. The weakest areas of any roof are the places where it changes direction or where one material (shingles, for instance) comes in contact with another (such as siding or metal flashing). It stands to reason that it's more expensive to replace a roof with many different planes, ridges, valleys, and features (such as skylights or chimneys) than to replace a simple peaked roof.

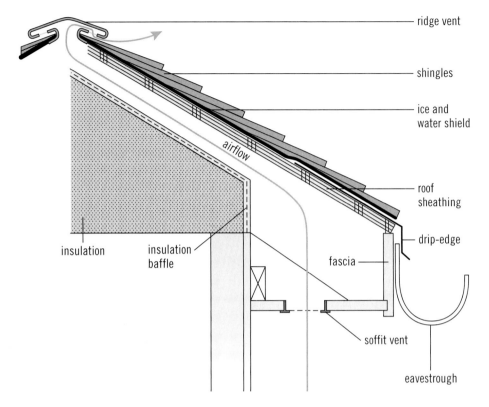

ridge vent

shingles

ice and
water shield

roof
sheathing

drip-edge

fascia

airflow

insulation

insulation
baffle

soffit vent

eavestrough

The roof is actually a system of components that gathers and directs rainwater, prevents ice buildup, and ventilates the attic. A drip-edge and bituminous membrane, very often referred to by the brand name "ice and water shield" should be part of a roof.The code rquires that all roofing be installed in accordance with the manufacturers' install-ation instructions. Many manufacturers require drip-edge to be installed. The code also requires "ice and water shield" where there has been a history of ice damming on roofs. It is a local determination, but it is provided for in the code.

Probably the biggest thing to look out for is too many layers on a roof. In most regions, minimum building code allows for two layers, but I think all re-roofing jobs should begin by removing old shingles and laying new ones on the plywood deck. (In some parts of the country that get a lot of hail, only one layer is allowed by code.) For one thing, that plywood needs to be made visible to judge whether it's still in good condition. For another, an extra layer of shingles adds a huge load to the roof, and once snow is added, the weight on the roof could actually cause it to collapse. Finally, moisture can get trapped between layers, causing rot and decay of the wood underneath. All in all, it's just a bad idea to keep shingling over the top of old layers, and I would be suspicious of the quality of any roof that has more than one layer.

Most of the time, home inspectors will inspect roofs from the ground or climb up a ladder to gutter level and make their roof examination from there. Whether an inspector is working from a ladder or from the ground, he should at least have binoculars to get a close-up view of the shingles, chimney, flashing, etc. You should ask the current owner about the age of the roof, but the proof is often right there in front of you, both on the inside (as visible water stains from the attic) and on the outside. The damage and wear are visible if you and the home inspector know the signs to look for. Replacing a roof is an expensive job, and you'll want to know how far off that job is before you put together an offer on any house.

ROOFING MATERIALS

ASPHALT SHINGLES

As you're house-hunting, you may encounter a huge variety of roofing materials, but odds are you will most often see roofs with asphalt shingles, which have been the most popular choice for roofs in North America for about 50 years. Made with fiberglass, paper, or felt impregnated with asphalt, they are covered in small mineral granules that reflect the ultraviolet rays of the sun, protecting the shingles to some degree. There are different levels of quality, ranging from "20-year shingles" to "35-year shingles." In my experience, none of them ever last that long.

 RED FLAGS FOR AN ASPHALT ROOF
- bare spots (mineral granules have fallen off and the shingle is left exposed)
- buckling in the middle of the shingle or curling at the edges. By the time you see this, the shingles don't have much lifetime left.
- large accumulations of granules in the gutters
- torn or missing shingles. The roof needs to be repaired or replaced right away.
- asphalt shingles being used on flat or nearly flat roofs. These shingles are meant for steeper pitches, and will leak like a sieve on flatter roofs.
- shingles improperly laid, with a continuous seam running up the slope. Water will get into this seam and cause damage to the roof deck — and everything else.
- two or more layers of shingles
- gobs of sealant or roofing tar (which can indicate past leaks)

WOOD SHINGLES AND SHAKES

Wood shingles and shakes can be made from redwood, cedar, or pine. They can be the thicker, hand-split variety (called shakes) or the somewhat thinner, machine-cut type (called shingles). Wood roofs look nice and they smell nice too, but they're not practical in all climates. They're expensive, they deteriorate from sun and rain, and repairing them can be expensive — you have to replace the whole roof. They are said to last between 30 and 50 years, but that's not what I've seen.

Roof "valleys" like this (top left) are where quality roofing is most important. The moss on this roof (top right) tells the story: this roof gets wet often and stays wet. Unless the roof has a very good water-and-ice shield (which is unlikely), rainwater is probably also forcing its way under the shingles and damaging the roof deck. A brand-new asphalt roof and gutter (bottom) have years of life ahead of them.

RED FLAGS FOR A WOOD SHINGLE OR SHAKE ROOF
- split, cupped, or curled shingles
- rot, particularly on lower shingles
- heavy moss or fungus growth, which indicates that shingles are not drying out properly after a rain (often seen on the north or shaded side of a roof)
- a low roof pitch (anything less than 4 in 12, even though code allows 3 in 12), which will speed up deterioration
- two or more layers of shingles
- gobs of sealant or roofing tar (which can indicate past leaks)

SLATE, CLAY TILE, AND CONCRETE TILE SHINGLES

Slate roofs were often used in the mid-Atlantic and northeastern parts of the U.S., and tile roofs are quite common in California and the southwestern U.S. Slate is probably the most expensive of all roofing materials, so it usually appears only on really elaborate Victorian homes. It was a prestige material back then, and it still is.

It adds value to a home. While slate roofing will last forever, the copper nails used to fasten it to the roof deck can fail due to oxidization, causing the tiles to slip off the roof and break. Careless walking on a slate roof can also break the pieces.

Clay tile (or Spanish tile) is also in the pricier range of roofing materials, and like slate, it adds value to a home. It's also very brittle, so it can break fairly easily — for instance, if a broken branch lands on the roof. Concrete tile shingles are designed to look like clay tile and can last 50 years or more.

What all these roofing materials have in common is that they are highly fire-resistant. They are also so heavy that the house has to be designed to carry the load. None of these materials should be used as a replacement roof without getting professional advice from an engineer about supporting the additional weight on the structure. If you are considering a home with these types of roofs, make sure you ask if the roof is original — if it's not, has the additional weight been accounted for in the structure?

 RED FLAGS FOR SLATE, CLAY TILE, AND CONCRETE TILE SHINGLES
- cracked, broken, or flaking shingles
- missing shingles
- visibly rusted nails on slate shingles
- any layering of these shingles with another type of shingle or roofing material

Cedar shingles look like this (top) when new. Unless they're treated with a weather-resistant stain (which is optional on cedar), they'll age to a silver color that many people like. Clay tiles (bottom) are still a premium material but are probably not the best long-term choice for cold climates.

METAL ROOFING

Metal is my favorite roofing material. It's relatively lightweight, extremely durable, fire-resistant, and it should last between 40 and 60 years. Metal roofs are about twice as expensive as asphalt roofs, but they will last about three times as long.

There are different kinds of metal roofs, of course. The traditional standing-seam roof, which was used for centuries on high-end houses, as well as on institutional and commercial buildings, was made of copper. Other metals used include galvanized steel, aluminum, and tin alloys; these are usually seen in rural areas on barns, and if they're not painted regularly, they will deteriorate.

RED FLAGS FOR OLDER METAL ROOFS
- punctures or tears
- peeling paint
- rust
- a steel roof combined with lead flashing around dormers or chimneys, which causes steel to deteriorate

The metal roofing used on houses today is usually steel. It can be applied as large individual shingles or as panels. These shingles or panels are formed to look, when installed, like traditional shingles, shakes, tile, or slate. The finish is a high-grade paint coating available in almost any color.

Steel is becoming a common roofing choice, but the added up-front cost means we're not yet seeing it used in large-scale housing developments. But as homeowners realize just how low-maintenance it is, and how long-lasting, it's likely to catch on in a big way.

Steel roofs are available in a range of styles and profiles, such as standing seam (left). Many metal roofs are installed in large panels, over wooden strapping (right).

FLAT OR BUILT-UP ROOFS

There really is no such thing as a flat roof — or there shouldn't be — since even so-called flat roofs have a slight pitch to allow water to run off into gutters and downspouts. And yesterday's flat roofs are a far cry from today's.

In the past, flat roofs were made using tar and gravel over a tarpaper surface. They didn't work very well. In fact, they leaked most of the time. The proof of a leaky flat roof is usually seen from the inside, as stains on ceilings (there usually isn't an attic under a flat roof). Wet spots can also be detected by using an infrared thermographic imaging camera.

 RED FLAGS FOR FLAT OR BUILT-UP ROOFS
- signs of leaks on the inside, especially on ceilings
- poor drainage, especially puddling, visible after a rain or when a hose is allowed to run on the roof during inspection
- bare spots where the gravel has been washed away
- visible tarpaper, especially paper that is dry, curling, or pulling away from the edge of the roof

Fortunately, better technologies than tar and gravel now exist for flat roofs. Not many houses are built with a flat roof these days, but if you find a new house with a roof like this — or a section of the roof — you will likely see a modified bitumen roof, There are two types of products: SBS, made from rubber, and APP, made from plastic It comes in rolls and can be torched down or mopped on using hot asphalt, and the seams are also torched to create a seamless membrane that is impervious to water. It is a high-quality type of roof that will last for 20 years or more if it's been properly installed.

Flat roofs aren't as common as they used to be, but the newer modified bitumen roofs, if properly installed, can last for 20 years or more.

CHIMNEYS

Chimneys, which are needed for both fireplaces and most types of furnaces, are a prime location for water problems that can cause serious structural damage. They are exposed to the elements; they are made of some type of stone or masonry (brick or concrete block) along with mortar, all of which are fire- and heat-resistant but likely to take on moisture; and they require proper sealing where the base of the chimney meets the roofing material.

A chimney should be examined from up close, which means climbing a ladder at the very least. That makes it a job for your home inspector only. Even from the ground, though, some problems will be obvious to you, once you know what you're looking for. Chimney problems can usually be repaired relatively cheaply, but they can turn into big problems if you leave them too long, and they are definitely safety hazards.

 RED FLAGS FOR CHIMNEYS
- inadequate, poorly installed, or non-existent metal flashing around the base. Roofing cement or tar is not enough to keep water from penetrating under the shingles and rotting the roof deck below.
- missing, cracked, or broken bricks
- gaps in the mortar. Repointing is needed or more deterioration will happen.
- a chimney that leans to one side, indicating that the mortar and bricks have not been maintained over the years
- parging (a skim coat of cement) to cover problem areas. Parging is not an adequate solution, and it will crack over time, allowing water in.
- a cracked or missing cap (usually made of concrete, flagstone, or steel), which should be like a miniature roof for the chimney itself, shedding water and keeping the masonry as dry as possible.
- inadequate chimney height in relation to the building. It should be 3 feet tall at a minimum, and it must be at least 2 feet higher than anything within 10 feet horizontally.
- dirty or blocked flues. The flue for a working fireplace should be cleaned every year, without exception.

A brick chimney needs to be examined for the quality of the bricks, mortar, chimney cap, and flashing. An old television antenna can cause damage to the brick and add more entry points for moisture.

ROOF VENTS AND GABLE VENTS

One sign of a good roofing job is how well it's ventilated. That's because roofs — and the attics under them — need to breathe, or they will decay quickly.

A good attic is properly sealed off from the living space below (with vapor barrier, insulation, and caulking) to keep humidity from getting into the attic and causing mold and other problems. The attic space is a cold zone (unless it's a finished attic, which is another story altogether; see Chapter 5) and it needs to be ventilated.

The minimum building code requirement is 1 square foot of roof vent (of any kind, whether ridge vents, gable vents, or other roof vents) for every 150 square feet of attic floor area. The most common type of roof vent is square, like a box, with one open side that faces the ground. The vent is usually color-coordinated with the roof but still very visible. The seal around it is critical, as is the quality of the vent itself.

Roof vents (top) and gable vents (left) are just two of the most common ways to move fresh air through attic spaces.

RED FLAGS FOR ROOF VENTS

- inadequate number of vents
- improper seal between vent and shingles
- dented or blocked vents. Birds' nests are a common cause of blockage.

I prefer to see ridge vents, which run continuously along the peak of the roof, or gable vents, which are louvered units set high up on the wall at both ends of a peaked roof. Either type will keep air moving through the attic almost all the time. Like any vent, gable vents have to be sealed correctly around the edges, but because they're on a vertical surface and don't require perforating the roof the way a roof vent does, they're less likely to let moisture in.

SKYLIGHTS

There's nothing like using a skylight to bring some extra sunlight into an interior room or windowless space. But especially with skylights, as with any product, the window is only as good as the installation. Think about it: you've got an opening in your roof — and we know that the roof is the easiest place for water to enter the house and do damage. The seal around a skylight has to be perfect, or you will have problems.

RED FLAGS FOR SKYLIGHTS

- single-glazed skylights. This means that the window has only one pane of glass, which is totally inadequate for any type of window.
- inadequate curbs. Skylights on roof slopes less than 3 in 12 need to have a 4" curb to shed water.
- a metal frame without a thermal break between the inner and outer surfaces. This will cause condensation, and eventually moisture damage.
- condensation between the panes of glass. The seal between the panes has been broken and the window will need replacing.
- interior water stains and other signs of leaking, such as peeling or bubbling paint, plaster, or drywall tape. Water is getting through this window and something will have to be done about it. The damage to the framing and other surrounding materials is probably even worse than what you can see inside the house.
- poorly installed or non-existent flashing around the exterior perimeter of the skylight. Flashing is absolutely necessary, because caulking alone will not do the job for longer than a year, or two at the most.
- skylights that don't open well, or at all. Some skylights are not meant to open and close (they are called inoperable, or fixed), but the ones that are designed to open should do so easily.

DORMERS

Like skylights, dormers interrupt the roofline and therefore are a potential source of water problems. They are also very difficult to insulate, which most people don't realize. The only kind of insulation I'd recommend for dormers is sprayed-on polyurethane, like Walltite, which gives you a vapor barrier and insulation as well as stopping air leakage.

The upside of dormers is easy enough to see: they give you more headroom and usable space in half-story rooms, and they add a lot of character to the house, both inside and out.

RED FLAGS FOR DORMERS

- missing, inadequate, or poorly installed flashing where dormer meets roofing material
- air leakage. In winter, if there is snow on some parts of the roof but not around the dormer, the dormer is probably allowing a lot of heat to escape — so much that it's melting the snow. In spring or fall, a heavy dew or frost will tell you something about the insulation around the dormer. A thermographic imaging camera will give you the best possible picture of heat loss around a dormer.
- stains and other signs of water damage on the interior, such as peeling plaster or drywall tape and rusted nails or screws showing through on drywalled corners

GUTTERS AND DOWNSPOUTS

Gutters and downspouts are the house's way of collecting and directing all the water or melting snow that gathers on the roof — which can be a lot more than you think. When they don't work right, they can be a source of water coming into the house at both the foundation level and the roof level. The condition they're in is a really good sign of how well the current owners have taken care of their house in general.

RED FLAGS FOR GUTTERS AND DOWNSPOUTS

- gutters clogged with leaves and other debris. If gutters are clogged, water will back up under the shingles and lead to ice damming and water damage to the roof deck in winter.
- disconnected sections of gutters, or gutters not properly connected to downspouts
- downspouts that empty too far from the ground or too close to the foundation without anything to catch and direct the water, such as splash blocks or rain barrels (rain barrels have to be emptied in the fall, of course, before the water has a chance to freeze)

This detail of a new house (top) shows just how many systems come together to form a gable: rooflines, flashing, soffits, fascia, gutters, brick veneer and even accent lighting in the eaves. These older homes (left and above) show the results of neglect.

What you don't want to see: Downspouts emptying onto a roof (above), or draining directly into the perimeter foundation drainbelow ground (left). The first will cause water and ice damage to the roof; the second could cause water damage to the foundation.

SOFFITS AND FASCIA

Soffits are the narrow horizontal sections under the roof eaves. Fascia are the front (outward-facing) part of the soffits, and usually have gutters attached to them. Older soffits were made of wood, while modern soffits are either aluminum or vinyl, with perforations that allow for ventilation. And that's the key issue with soffits — do they allow air into the attic? Even when there are other roof vents, soffit vents are critical for enough airflow to keep attics dry.

 RED FLAGS FOR SOFFITS AND FASCIA
- solid wood soffits without ventilation. Older wood soffits require regular painting and could be rotting, as well.
- perforated aluminum soffits over old solid wood soffits. If holes haven't been drilled in the wood to allow air to flow through, the perforated soffits are useless. This requires careful inspection.
- more than one layer of aluminum or vinyl. When soffits are nailed over the top of each other, ventilation is impossible.
- no baffles to take the air through the insulation and into the air space of the attic. These are necessary to get soffit vents working right. Your home inspector should be checking this out from inside the attic.

The key question with soffits, old or new, is whether they allow air into the attic.

STRUCTURE AND SHEATHING: THE BONES AND SKIN OF EVERY HOUSE

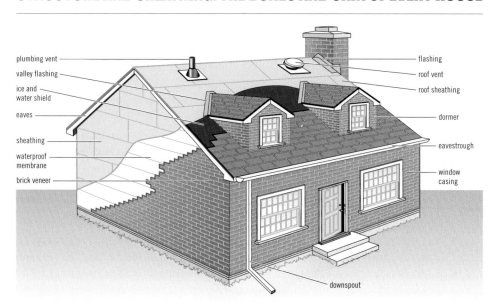

plumbing vent
valley flashing
ice and water shield
eaves
sheathing
waterproof membrane
brick veneer

flashing
roof vent
roof sheathing
dormer
eavestrough
window casing

downspout

FOUNDATION

Ever gone for a drive in the country and seen an old barn leaning to one side, looking like it was about five minutes from falling over? Chances are, what you saw was the result of a foundation that had finally lost its footing — literally. And though most houses are built on better foundations than aging barns are, houses and barns have this in common: structural walls are only as strong as the foundation that holds them up. If the foundation begins to crumble and sag, the rest of the structure will follow.

You can see why it's important to assess the solidity and strength of any foundation. The starting point for almost any foundation is undisturbed earth — ground that has been compacted over thousands or millions of years. Solid ground, in other words, that won't allow the house to shift as it settles. The first part of the foundation is the footing, which rests on that undisturbed ground, and is usually about twice the width of the walls that sit on it. (Exceptions are very old buildings like that barn, which probably had nothing more than a stone foundation that widened at the bottom to provide some extra support.) There are footings under the entire perimeter of the house (the exterior walls), and also footings of some kind under a center wall or posts. Of course, you'll never see the footings of a house, but you might see the foundation cracks that come from a bad footing, or other problems with walls that show the footing might be sinking.

The other factor you're looking for in a foundation is how well it protects against moisture. As with every other part of our exterior structure, we want the foundation to keep the water on the outside. If the foundation of a house is exposed to water over a long enough period of time without adequate protection, the pressure that's exerted by the ground water will push its way through almost any building material. The dampness eventually results in mold and rot when the water comes in contact with building materials made of wood (such as framing studs) or paper (such as drywall). In the worst cases, the force of the water will even cause the walls to buckle.

You should examine the foundation from both the outside and the inside (the basement), but for the moment, while you're walking around the perimeter of the house, you and your home inspector are going to make an initial assessment from the outside.

First of all, what kind of foundation is it? There are a number of possibilities. The four main types are full foundation, partial foundation (crawl space), slab-on-grade foundation, and open foundation.

In the Eastern and Midwestern parts of the U.S., most homes have a full foundation. From the inside, a full foundation creates a full-height basement. It can be made in a number of ways and using a variety of building materials.

Fieldstone and even brick were commonly used in the past (especially prior to the twentieth century). Both can be problematic because the ratio of stone or brick to mortar is so high: mortar isn't as strong, and, like brick itself, it's very absorbent. Builders at the time knew this would be the case, so these foundations were built very thick to allow for the water to dissipate as it moved through the wall. In those days basements were expected to be damp places, and no one thought of them as living space.

Brick foundations aren't that common anymore, and this photo shows why: the porous brick absorbs water and breaks down badly over time. Some amateur parging has been attempted here, and a low concrete ledge has been added for strength and stability.

Poured concrete has been the most common type of foundation since about the 1920s, along with concrete block (also called cinder block) and pre-cast concrete sections. Concrete is somewhat more impervious to moisture, but all three of these materials will absorb water, which can cause problems on the inside of the house. Until recently, protecting the foundation against moisture has been the most overlooked part of the equation, and we're finding that a lot of houses need to have the area around the foundation excavated in order to do a proper job of waterproofing. (Unfortunately, even new homes are not usually well enough waterproofed around the foundation.)

More recently, an excellent new system called insulated concrete forms (ICF) has been gaining popularity for foundations. (In fact, they can be used to build the entire house, not just the foundation.) These forms are made of rigid foam with an insulation value of R-25; they have hollow centers and fit together a lot like Lego pieces. First they are reinforced with rebar (metal rods), then concrete is poured into the hollow centers, creating a perfectly straight wall with a built-in vapor barrier and insulation. An extra layer of moisture protection is usually added on the exterior; ideally, it will be a seamless foundation coating that resembles an enormous elastic band wrapped around the foundation. It stretches and moves with the structure, and it's totally waterproof. Finally, a dimpled black plastic product is wrapped around the foundation as a secondary barrier to help protect the waterproofing system. Altogether, this system is a great investment, and if you come across a newer house built using ICF, you're in luck.

A partial foundation means that the foundation is only about 4 or 5 feet deep — just deep enough to go past the frost line in the ground but not deep enough to make a real basement. Foundations like this can be built using any of the materials and methods mentioned above for full foundations.

The outer layer of parging — concrete, stucco, or mortar that's troweled on — is crumbling away on this concrete foundation (above left), but it's not a sign that the structure is at risk. A new foundation (right) shows the black dimpled plastic that is commonly used by builders as part of a two-stage waterproofing system.

A slab-on-grade foundation is just that — a concrete slab, usually a couple of feet thick and reinforced with steel bars, that's resting on solid ground. It still requires a footing of at least 18" (4' is better). It should be properly insulated and protected from moisture underneath with a layer of rigid foam board over gravel. When a slab foundation is built incorrectly — without proper footings, for example — it can be really bad news, especially in a cold climate, where frost causes heaving of the soil. Many additions today are built over crawl spaces (partial foundations) or slabs.

Once in a while, especially with cottages and some older homes, you'll see an open foundation. This means that a number of posts or piers have been dug into the ground and the house has been set on top of them. This is a faster, cheaper way of building, but sometimes it can also be the best way — I've heard of cottages being built on the solid rock of the Canadian Shield (which is cottage country for many people in Ontario), and piers drilled into the rock make a lot of sense.

One of the challenges of an open foundation is that the underside of the house is hard to insulate adequately, and it's hard to protect it from moisture and animals.

RED FLAGS FOR FOUNDATIONS

- an uneven roofline. If there are problems with settling or sinking of the foundation, you'll see it in a sagging roofline (or floors, once you get inside).
- foundation walls that buckle, bulge, or lean in any direction. The foundation is shifting because of water pressure from poor drainage or poor waterproofing, inadequate or sinking footings, or modifications to the structure that have been done wrong and have compromised the foundation.
- major cracks of a ¼ inch or more, especially if the cracks run in more than one direction or if they extend up into exterior walls of brick, stone, or stucco. When cracks have been a problem for a long time, you may see signs of patching and painting. You likely need expert advice to determine if the house is still settling and shifting or if the movement has stopped and will not cause any more problems.
- wood in contact with the soil. Moisture damage and insects (especially termites) are the big concern here. Only pressure-treated wood can safely touch soil, but not as part of the foundation,
- basement windows that extend below grade (ground level) or within 4 inches of ground level and that are not fitted with properly drained window wells

- for pier foundations, not enough piers for the spans, and any piers no longer fully in contact with the structure or with the ground below. The piers may not have been sunk deep enough into the soil, or the soil underneath may have settled since the piers were put in place. Either way, these are serious problems that need to be addressed.
- any new or enlarged window or door. The structure must be supported properly or the new opening will introduce a domino effect of problems. Always ask to see building permits and inspection approvals.

As I always maintain, in a renovation, anything can be fixed and anything is possible. But if you're already stretching your budget to buy a new house, ask yourself how much you can really afford for major renovations like foundation repair. Foundation work is expensive and invisible — which makes it the kind of work that most people don't enjoy paying for.

If you and your home inspector suspect that a house has serious foundation problems but you're still interested in buying it, call in an expert to get a true evaluation. The cost of a few hours with a structural engineer or foundation specialist will be money well spent.

EXTERIOR WALLS

Foundation walls extend upward into exterior walls. Most of the time, exterior walls are built with a wood frame and then an exterior skin is added, such as siding, stucco, or brick veneer. Solid brick houses are another possibility. Wood frame construction has become the most popular because wood is readily available, and the process of building with 2×4 studs (or 2×6s) allows a

Exterior walls in most of today's new home construction begin with wood framing and sheathing.

natural space for insulation, wiring, and plumbing.

A traditional method of building frame houses is called balloon framing, which means that the studs of the house go all the way from the foundation walls up to the roofline, and the floors are hung from those studs. In a balloon-framed house without insulation, you could drop a marble down the wall cavity from the attic and it would only hit bottom at the foundation sill. (An exception to this would be balloon-framed walls that have wood blocks called firestops nailed between studs at several locations.)

Today, most houses are built using platform framing, which means that each level is built individually, in sections. When one level is done, another platform is added above it to create the floor of the next level.

You can't tell from the exterior what type of framing has been used — although the age of the house is some indication — but in fact it shouldn't matter much, since they're about the same in terms of strength.

What you're looking for on the outside is the type and quality of the veneer or skin — the siding, stucco, brick, etc. Some materials are more desirable than others, both from an aesthetic point of view and in terms of durability. Let's look at the various possibilities.

WOOD SIDING (CLAPBOARD OR BOARD-AND-BATTEN)

Wood is where siding began, not only in North America but also in Europe, hundreds of years ago. Some of the most admired old Victorian houses are made of wood siding (often called clapboard), and board-and-batten (vertical siding) also has its proponents.

But even its devotees will admit that wood is prone to decay and rot,

Painted wood siding requires constant maintenance. Peeling is inevitable.

and to date no one has been able to develop a paint for wood that can really withstand the realities of extreme temperatures, rain, snow, sun, wind — and the expansion and contraction of the wood itself. Penetrating stains are an improvement (they fade rather than flake), but they still need to be redone every five years or so.

RED FLAGS FOR WOOD SIDING
- flaking, peeling, and bubbling paint
- wood rot and decay, particularly close to the ground and around windows and doors
- siding that extends too close to the ground (8 inches is the closest it should ever get, though code allows 6 inches)

Aluminum and vinyl siding, with their lower cost and lower maintenance, try to imitate wood, and for the most part they've taken over where wood left off. Whatever their qualities, though, they aren't seen as premium products, so in some higher-end neighborhoods especially, they don't add huge value to a house.

There are wood products now available that seem to offer the best of both worlds. Pre-stained wood siding (in cedar, fir, or pine) is about twice as expensive as vinyl or aluminum, but it is factory-finished and usually has a 15-year warranty on the stain, along with a 50-year warranty on the wood itself. For people who love wood or who want to buy a product made from completely renewable resources, wood siding can be a reasonable choice.

The looks and historical value of some older painted wooden houses are what makes them worth all the maintenance.

ALUMINUM SIDING

From about the 1960s to the 1980s, aluminum was the standard in siding. It was meant to imitate traditional clapboard (wood) siding, but it was supposed to be more durable and maintenance-free — and it was cheaper by far than replacing or even maintaining the existing wood, which had to be painted every couple of years.

RED FLAGS FOR ALUMINUM SIDING

- dents and scratches
- faded or worn finish, especially when greyish aluminum is visible underneath
- missing, cracked, or gaping caulking around corner and window trim, which allow moisture to get behind the siding

VINYL SIDING

Vinyl siding has been around since the 1960s, but it didn't get much attention until the '70s, and it really came into its own in the '80s. For many years, it was used only to update or refurbish older frame houses, but in recent years it's become one of the most popular exterior finishes for new homes as well, often used with brick veneer to reduce the overall building costs.

RED FLAGS FOR VINYL SIDING

- cracked, broken or loose siding
- mildew, which signals water problems that may go behind the siding, as well
- missing, cracked, or gaping caulking around corner and window trim, which allow moisture to get behind the siding

STUCCO

Stucco got a bad reputation a long time ago because it has a history of cracking and falling apart. There are a couple of reasons why that happens. To start with, stucco (a mixture of Portland cement, sand, lime, and water) is like brick, mortar, and concrete: it's porous and absorbs water. It's most durable in climates where the temperatures are fairly constant, or at least constantly above freezing, because the freezing and thawing are what cause stucco to expand and contract — and then break apart.

What makes the problem worse is when stucco is applied right over wood siding, with only wire mesh to hold it in place. Wood moves a lot with changes in temperature and humidity, so the stucco on a wood house ends up with a lot of small cracks. Then moisture gets into those cracks and causes everything to break down. If stucco is applied to a wood house, the only way to do it right is to use rigid foam insulation boards on the walls first, and then apply the stucco on top. Ideally, stucco is used on masonry or ICF walls (insulated concrete forms), which won't move.

RED FLAGS FOR TRADITIONAL STUCCO

- cracks, either minor or major, especially around windows, doors, corners, and joins of any kind
- heaving of the stucco. Test this by pressing against the wall and by looking for any areas that seem to be bulging outwards.
- wet areas on the wall after a rain. The best time to inspect stucco is after a rainfall, because areas that remain very wet indicate that the stucco is holding moisture.
- on a Tudor-style house, where stucco is used in combination with wood as a surface material, look for areas where water has collected and caused the wood to rot.

A newer generation of cement-based stucco is now on the market, and it's an improvement on the first. Acrylic-based stuccos are also available, but they can trap moisture and cause damage to the wood framing members. They're better in dry climates, such as the southwest United States, or strictly over rigid foam, not wood.

WOOD SHINGLES OR SHAKES

Wood shingles or shakes are usually made of cedar, and they are installed the same way that cedar shakes and shingles would be installed on a roof, except they are on a completely vertical surface. Because walls are vertical, they tend to shed water better than roofs, and wood shingles therefore often last longer on exterior walls. They can be left natural, stained, or painted. Painted shingles will require more maintenance than any other treatment.

RED FLAGS FOR WOOD SHINGLES OR SHAKES

- loose, damaged, split, or missing shingles
- moss, fungus, or other signs of rot

FIBER CEMENT SIDING

Fiber cement siding is one of the newer siding products on the market, and so far it looks like a good bet. This siding looks like wood, but it's actually a mixture of cement, sand, and cellulose fibers. Even though it's more expensive and time-consuming to install than either aluminum or vinyl, because it's cheaper than wood, fiber cement is being used in many parts of the U.S. on new homes.

Fiber cement siding often comes pre-primed In the Eastern and Midwestern parts of the U.S. It has to be painted or stained within about three months of installation or it might start to show signs of breaking down. Manufacturers claim that it will hold paint and stain for about seven to 15 years. As with many products, the key to success is in the installation.

 RED FLAGS FOR FIBER CEMENT SIDING
- nails driven below the surface (this reduces holding power)
- wooden exterior casings on windows, doors, and corners. There's nothing wrong with wood trim, but it should be maintained with paint or capped with aluminum. Otherwise it will deteriorate at a much faster rate than cement-board siding.
- waviness in the walls is a sign of poor installation or a problem with the structure underneath.

Wood shingles have a longer life when they're used on exterior walls rather than rooftops.

ASPHALT SHINGLES (INSULBRICK)

From about the 1940s to the 1970s, asphalt shingles were used as a siding material. The hope was that they would give some insulating value and be low-cost and maintenance-free. But they had almost no insulating value, and the imitation brick look didn't fool anyone. You won't see anyone applying insulbrick these days — in fact, it's almost impossible to find because it's no longer being made — but you will often see it being covered up by some other form of siding.

Because insulbrick is now such an undesirable material and it actually detracts from the value of a house, you might say that its presence is a red flag in itself. But it can be removed, so you may be able to get a good deal on the house to begin with and then make a sow's ear into a silk purse. Be sure to have a professional remove the material, because it may contain asbestos.

This insulbrick (which is a brand name that's become generic for siding made from a tar-impregnated mat embossed with a brick pattern) has decayed along the bottom edge, close to the foundation, exposing the wood sheathing underneath.

SOLID BRICK OR BRICK VENEER

Brick is seen as one of the most durable and desirable exterior finishes. But all brick houses are not equal. There are two main possibilities: solid masonry and brick veneer.

Solid masonry construction, found mostly in older homes, is sometimes called double brick because it uses two layers (or wythes) of brick, with or possibly without a wood frame. In older homes, the inner layer of bricks was covered with wooden lath and plaster, then covered with oil paint to block any further moisture from coming through the wall.

Sometimes — though not always — double-brick walls are held together with a header row of bricks, usually every six rows. The header bricks appear to be half the size of the other bricks, but in reality they're just turned ninety degrees, so what you're seeing is the end of the brick. Header rows are usually a sign that you're looking at double-brick construction.

Brick veneer, on the other hand, is actually a single layer of full-size, full-thickness brick built on a wood-frame house. In newer houses (and some older ones) you'll often find brick veneer. One way you can sometimes spot brick veneer is by looking at the sides of the house. If the front is brick but the sides and back are covered in siding of some kind, you know the front is not there for structural support and that it's only a single layer thick.

Wood framing is the starting point for most brick houses today. The bricks form the outer layer only, which is why it's called brick veneer.

RED FLAGS FOR BRICK AND BRICK VENEER

- cracks in bricks or mortar. This is more serious in solid brick houses because the bricks may be structural. In brick veneer houses, it works the other way around: the house holds up the brick. Cracks in bricks and mortar usually follow directly from cracks in the foundation. They need to be evaluated very carefully to determine the cause and the possibilities and cost of repair. Hairline cracks above doors and windows are not usually serious.
- missing or crumbling mortar. The bricks are more susceptible to moisture damage, and repointing (chiseling out and replacing the mortar) is necessary.
- improperly raked mortar. Many new homes are built very quickly and it shows in the mortar work. Mortar should be concave and flush with the brick so that water runs out of the mortar. If water pools in the mortar, the water can freeze and damage the bricks around it.
- signs of settling or sloping. The brick veneer could be coming away from the framing and may need to be completely rebuilt.
- vines climbing on a brick wall. These look beautiful, no doubt about it, but they can damage the mortar and allow moisture to penetrate deep into both bricks and mortar.

MIKE'S TIPS
Points for brick maintenance

Brick seems like the ultimate low-maintenance exterior. And when you consider how long it lasts, it probably is. One thing that does need to be maintained, though, is the mortar between the bricks. Crumbling mortar and loose bricks let in water. Pointing (also called tuck-pointing or repointing) involves scraping out the old mortar and adding new. This has to be done by someone with skill and experience. An amateur job will look terrible and should be very obvious to an inspector.

The cost of tuck-pointing is labor, not materials, so some guys will try to take a shortcut and put the new mortar over top of the old. Code doesn't address tuckpointing, but according to American Society for Testing and Materials (ASTM): Proper preparation of mortar joints should include the removal of old mortar to a minimum depth of two to three times the width of the joint to ensure an adequate bond and performance of the mortar. With joints typically being 3/8 in. (10 mm) wide in most brick masonry, this requires removing existing mortar to a depth of at least 3/4 in. (20 mm) from the face of the masonry. There is a caulking on the market that is supposed to be a replacement for tuck-pointing, but I don't recommend it except as a quick fix to stop water from penetrating the mortar. Stick with mortar or cement and ask about having a liquid bonder added to the mix. The bonder, which looks like milk, will help the new mortar stick to the old brick.

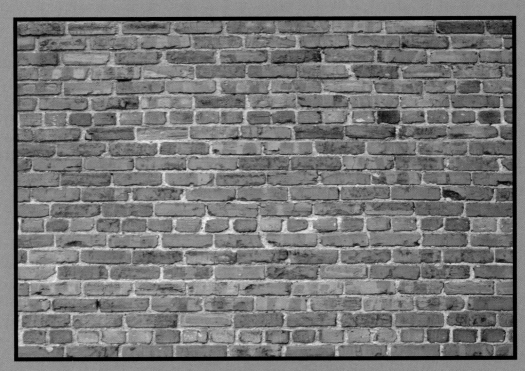

GARAGE

If the house you're looking at actually has a garage, especially in a high-density city where space for parking (and everything else) is at a premium, you're already ahead. Even if it's a small, rundown detached garage on a back alley, if you want to replace it, you'll have an easier time getting a permit to replace an existing building than to build from nothing. In any case, garages of almost any kind are considered a major selling feature.

For attached garages, an important factor to keep in mind is that there must be an adequate gas barrier between the garage and the living spaces of the house. This requirement is in the building code for safety reasons: you don't want carbon monoxide and fumes from gasoline or other toxic chemicals stored there to enter the house. In any event, the garage itself should be drywalled, plastered and caulked where required. It shouldn't be difficult if the interior wall has both proper insulation and a vapor barrier, though it could pose a problem in older, uninsulated houses.

 RED FLAGS FOR GARAGES
- non-existent gas barrier on walls between garage and house
- non-existent or inadequate fireproof door to house
- inadequate size for number of vehicles or for storage needs
- garage door opening is too small for your vehicles to enter safely and easily
- garage door does not open smoothly, or stay open
  If the automatic garage door opener doesn't plug directly into an outlet. Using an extension cord violates National Electrical Code.

This double-width garage door should be examined for proper installation and smooth functioning.

PORCH, DECK, OR BALCONY

Almost everyone sees a deck, veranda, or some other form of outdoor living space as a selling feature. That's fine, but you want to verify how well these structures are built, whether there's contact between wood and the ground (an invitation to insects, especially termites), and how much maintenance they'll require.

 RED FLAGS FOR A PORCH, DECK, OR BALCONY
- very old, rotting structures. Look closely at steps, railings, and joints. They might look nice on the surface but not have much usable life left.
- contact between wood and the soil. Wood rot can be just that, or it could be a sign that insects are at work.
- structure improperly attached to the main building, although sometimes decks are built as freestanding structures on their own pier foundation.

Having a wide front porch (above) is like having an outdoor living room. On a newer home (left), a deck is supported by a beam made of three boards sistered together, which rest on a 6×6 post.

1. INSULATION

If the house was built before World War I, and probably even up to the 1950s, it likely has no insulation at all. The technology just didn't exist, or wasn't being used in houses very much. The best they could do before that was create air pockets in the wall cavities, which was some help, but not much. There are ways to add insulation to an older home, working from either the exterior or interior, but they are generally expensive.

2. VAPOR BARRIER

There is no vapor barrier on older houses. In the past, it was expected that moisture would work its way into the walls and back out again. Oil-based paints provided the same protection for plaster walls as a 2-mil sheet of vapor barrier plastic would do today. The code requires vapor retarders, which are dependent on the climate and classified by their perm rating--a measurement of how readily moisture passes through a material.

3. BUILDING CODES

Bringing an older house up to today's minimum building code standards can create new problems, especially with moisture.

4. WIRING

Old houses usually contain knob-and-tube wiring. Not a problem if it's used correctly (without overloading the fuses), except that it's rarely insurable these days. And modifications have almost always been made to older wiring, which raises the possibility that they've been tied in badly. Even where it looks like the wiring is completely new, you should be suspicious. Ask for permits and inspection reports on all electrical work.

5. BRICK ISSUES

Brick homes that have been sandblasted may give you big problems. Contrary to most people's expectations, brick is actually a very porous material. But it does have a thin outer coat that seals and protects it to some degree. When brick has been painted or gotten dirty over time, some people try the sandblasting route. The blasted brick looks great—fresher and cleaner than it's been for a long time—but it's now exposed to the elements like never before. It will deteriorate quickly after sandblasting and could introduce a lot of moisture-related problems.

6. DRAINAGE

In an older home, proper grading away from the house is especially important, since it may never have had any form of drainage system around the foundation. Even if the foundation does have a perforated pipe system, the tiles may be cracked, broken, or filled with dirt or roots by this time. You'll need to keep the water flowing away from the house and be prepared for moisture problems in the basement at any time unless you undertake a complete excavation and waterproofing project.

7. BASEMENTS

Basements in older homes were not intended as living space. They were meant to get wet. That sounds strange, but to the people who built these houses a hundred years ago or more, it would seem at least as strange to want to use your basement for a bar and a wide-screen TV. Foundations were thick so that moisture could dissipate as it moved through the stone or concrete, but there was no exterior waterproofing. Making an older foundation and basement waterproof can be a big and expensive job, and you have to choose your contractor very carefully: not enough of them know how to do it right. For new construction, code merely requires basement damp-proofing, unless there is a very high water table in your area.

8. VINES

Brick covered with vines looks pretty, but vines can create real problems. Whether they're growing over wood siding or brick, they can make maintenance impossible. An even bigger problem is that the vines actually force their way into wood, brick, and mortar, letting moisture in. The wall may look fantastic, but the bricks could be crumbling. Vines can also give insects very easy access to the house.

9. FLOORS

Old hardwood floors will probably have at least a slight slope to them, and they will probably creak. These things happen over time as the house settles and the wood dries out. Floors can be straightened—sometimes. Hardwood can be made to stop creaking—maybe. If you can't stand sloping, creaking floors, you'd better avoid old houses.

10. HERITAGE DESIGNATIONS

If an older home has been given a historic designation or is in a historic district, the town may have restrictions on what its owner can do to the exterior. If you buy an older house property, be prepared for limitations and for a layer or two of bureaucracy every time you want to change or upgrade something on your home. The interiors of heritage houses aren't usually affected by these rules.

WHAT'S IT GOING TO COST?

If you are considering a home that needs some work or if you have big dreams, it's easy to underestimate how much that renovation could cost. Here are some rough cost estimates — the only way to know how much something actually will cost, of course, is to get detailed estimates from reliable contractors.

ROOF

Project	Rough Cost Range	Good to Know
asphalt	$0.50–$2.50/sq. ft. (shingles only; installation extra)	Although minimum code allows two layers of asphalt shingles, always insist on one layer when replacing your roof so you can inspect the roof sheathing. Always keep the bag from one package of shingles for warranty purposes.
flat (modified bitumen)	$8–$12/sq. ft (installed)	
flat (conventional felt-and-gravel built-up roof)	$6–$10/sq. ft. (installed)	
flat (EPDM: single-ply rubber membrane)	$6–$10/sq. ft. (installed)	
flat (TPO: polyolefin)	$6–$10/sq. ft. (installed)	
metal	$5.50–$10/sq. ft. (installed)	Metal roofs may cost more upfront, but they last longer and are fireproof.

FOUNDATION

Project	Rough Cost Range	Good to Know
repairs and waterproofing	varies widely	Foundation repairs can be complex and expensive. If you spot a problem with a foundation in a house you're considering, be careful, and bring in a specialist for another opinion.

EXTERIOR FINISHING

Project	Rough Cost Range	Good to Know
tuckpointing brick	$5–$15/sq. ft. * (depending on condition of brick and mortar)	When tuckpointing, at least 3/4" of old mortar needs to be chiseled out before putting in new mortar.
vinyl siding	$1.50–$3 sq. ft. * (materials only; labor extra)	
wood siding	$1.50–$5 sq. ft. * (materials only)	
fiber cement siding	$3–$6 sq. ft. * (materials only)	Fiber cement board is one of the most durable kinds of siding, but it still needs some maintenance.

* cost per square foot of exterior surface

FENCE

Project	Rough Cost Range	Good to Know
cedar	$15–$20/lin. ft.	Post holes need to be at least 4' deep to prevent frost heave. Pros also make sure that the tops of the holes aren't feathered and scoop out the bottom of the hole for added protection.
pressure-treated	$10–$15/lin. ft.	

DECK

Project	Rough Cost Range	Good to Know
cedar deck boards	$25-$35/sq. ft.	Decks more than 30" above the ground need a permit, although some towns require a permit for any deck.
pressure-treated deck boards	$20-$30/sq. ft.	To save money, you can use pressure-treated wood for the structure and cedar for the decking only.
custom	The sky's the limit.	Always think about safety — build proper railings.

CHAPTER FOUR
The Basement and Mechanicals

"To gain more space for our growing family, we decided to get started on the basement. I removed the previous owner's so-called partially finished basement. As the uneven paneled walls came down, there were things there that made my heart stop … Mike, there are about 40 rod holes exposed and 11 massive cracks (one is 16 feet long), and 'honeycomb' concrete throughout. Next I observed the floor joists, some of which are two pieces, not one, from end to end. I went outside and saw that the foundation wall on one side is not even flush with the brick, but someone parged it to appear even. Tall flowers were placed outside to hide stairway cracks. Shouldn't our home inspector have noticed these things?"

—A.R.

Along with the exterior, the basement is where you'll find answers to key questions about the house — key money questions.

After looking at so many details on the exterior, and before we look through the main-floor rooms, we need to go downstairs to the basement. If the kitchen is the heart of the house, the basement is where you find the guts — the internal organs that make the whole thing function.

The basement gives us more evidence about the condition of the structure, which we looked at pretty extensively from the outside, and lots of information about the mechanicals — the electrical, plumbing, and HVAC (heating, ventilation, and air conditioning) — which are the areas of your house that ultimately will cost you the most to fix or upgrade.

Because those areas are so important, I suggest hiring several professionals, in addition to the home inspector, to help you do a thorough evaluation. A licensed electrician, a licensed plumber, and a licensed HVAC specialist are all needed if you really want to know whether the mechanicals are up to scratch.

When I inspect a house, I always hope to find an unfinished basement. For one thing, it's easier to see all the mechanicals when the walls and ceiling are exposed instead of closed in with drywall. For another, a finished basement is too often finished badly — most of the time, moisture is being trapped in the walls and the floor. When that's the case, you'll be paying a premium for the "selling feature" of a finished basement, but you may well have to rip it out before long and start over again. Then that selling feature ends up costing you double.

You'll probably encounter some finished basements while you're house hunting. Let me explain why I have serious questions whenever I see a finished basement and what you should watch out for.

WHY ARE THERE SO MANY PROBLEMS WITH FINISHED BASEMENTS?

Finishing a basement sounds simple enough. Just about every home handyman has done one or helped out with one, and many people have spent thousands and thousands of dollars hiring contractors to make a dream basement for them. The problem is that not enough people — not even some contractors — know how to do it right. Here are some areas of concern:

1. MOISTURE

The key thing, as with so many other parts of building right, is how to keep things dry. The basement is below ground. The walls of a basement — the foundation — are made of concrete, cinder block or stone. No matter what the material, they all let at least some water through, especially since the pressure of the water surrounding the foundation is constantly pushing moisture through. Under the concrete floor (which in older homes may be only a couple of inches thick, or even less) you may have the risk of a high water table forcing moisture up through it.

But here's the key problem: In a finished basement with a height of somewhere between 6 and 8 feet (depending on the house), the temperature at floor level is between 60° and 68° Farenheit. However, since most basements finish above ground, the temperature near the ceiling (on the underside of the floor joists) is prone to change according to the weather outside. So, in the summer it's warmer, and in the winter it's colder. That temperature difference means that if there is any airflow against the concrete or cinder-block wall, there will be moisture condensation. Guaranteed.

Wood will absorb moisture from the concrete (moisture can also attack metal framing, but I simply wouldn't use it in a basement). The framing cavity gets filled with batt insulation and then a 6-mil plastic-sheet vapor barrier is applied — and now the real problems start. An air pocket is formed behind the vapor barrier, with two different air masses in constant play. In the summer, find a finished basement built to code, poke a hole in it, and I guarantee you the insulation will be wet.

The place to solve water problems is on the outside of the house. In many older homes — and too many new ones — that wasn't done. When those older homes were built, the technology didn't exist to keep the foundation dry, and in many cases it may be very difficult and expensive to excavate around the house and fix the problem. In newer homes, most builders are doing their best to make foundations waterproof, but they also want to get away with the minimum that the building code allows, which is dampproofing, not waterproofing. It's cheaper that way, of course, but it isn't good enough to guarantee a dry basement.

So we're left with many houses that have some degree of moisture in the basement — sometimes visible and sometimes invisible. But the basement still seems to be the most logical place to get that extra space that everybody wants. Just put up some studs on the walls, add insulation and drywall, and you're done, right? How about a carpet to warm up that cold concrete floor? Done this way, a basement will look fine for a year or two, even three if you're lucky. After that, the moisture will let you know it's there — with mildew, that musty smell, maybe even some mushroom-like growths in the corners and on the carpet. There comes a point when you have to tear everything out and start over again.

Better to do it right the first time.

To finish a basement properly, you have to address moisture coming from the outside and the temperature differences inside that cause moisture. For both a thermal break and a vapor barrier on the walls, I recommend 2" rigid foam board insulation glued directly to the walls with the proper foam adhesive, with all gaps filled with spray foam and the seams covered with polypropylene tape with acrylic adhesive. Tuck-Tape and Venture tape are two well-known brands.. This gives you the starting point for studs, electrical, plumbing, and drywall. Anything less won't do the job.

Likewise, for the floor you need a thermal break and a vapor barrier before you put down finish flooring. Painted concrete, sealed concrete, vinyl or linoleum over concrete — these are all surefire ways to keep a concrete floor from breathing. Carpet, especially if it's laid with glue (mastic) of any kind, is another no-go. Hardwood? Don't even think about it unless the floor has first been made moisture-tight with 1" rigid foam board insulation float-

The first step to finishing a basement should be adding rigid foam board insulation to the walls, which forms both a thermal break and vapor barrier.

ing to the floor. Follow this with a layer of ⅝" tongue-and-groove plywood screwed into the concrete with self-tapping concrete screws made by Tapcon, and your floor will be ready to take any type of finish flooring you like — even hardwood.

2. STRUCTURE

The project of finishing a basement often involves enlarging windows or adding entrances. These are major structural changes that must be done right or they will threaten the structural integrity of the home. Again, if any changes like this have been done, demand to see permits and inspection reports. And if the basement has a bedroom but there are no doors to the outside or windows large enough to escape through in a fire, you have a safety issue as well as a code violation — and some evidence that there are probably no permits or inspections to see.

3. HEATING, VENTILATION, AND AIR CONDITIONING

Furnaces and air-conditioning systems are designed to heat a certain amount of space. A finished basement increases the amount of space that the furnace needs to heat. It takes at least one vent opening from the heating ducts and at least one cold air return.

Adding finished floor space with a basement renovation generally requires an HVAC specialist to balance your forced air system so that there is adequate airflow throughout the basement.

4. PLUMBING

If there's a bathroom, kitchen, or bar sink in the basement, you want to make sure it's been vented properly. Too many people try to cram bathrooms into basements without making sure that the venting conforms at least to minimum code. The result is poor drainage for the life of that bathroom. A licensed plumber should be able to advise you.

5. ELECTRICAL

It seems that some of the worst electrical work I've seen is in basements that are finished out later. A lot of basements are finished off without getting building permits, seeing as how the work is out of view and the noise of construction is muffled. Poor design and workmanship and use of the wrong materials create unsafe conditions that you can't see.

HOW CAN YOU TELL IF A FINISHED BASEMENT WAS FINISHED RIGHT?

Your nose knows a lot.

The first indication of a problem basement will probably be a bad, musty smell. That's a sure sign there is moisture in the basement. And that smell might also be telling you that there's a mold problem.

Sometimes you can actually see or feel signs of moisture as well. Can you see mildew or mold growing anywhere? Look closely in corners, at the wall near the floor, and on any exterior walls. Can you see nails popping out of drywall, especially rusty nails? When you're walking around in your socks on a carpeted basement floor (carpet being the most popular choice for finished basements), do your feet feel damp?

The basement is the zone of the house where a thermal imaging camera would be most useful. I hope it won't be too long before all building and home inspectors use these cameras, because they truly allow us to look behind walls. And what they do particularly well is show us moisture — where it's totally invisible to the naked eye. If your home inspector has a thermal imaging camera, make sure he uses it and explains to you exactly what he's seeing.

You also want to look at the finishing touches — how well the trim and molding around windows and doors have been done, for example — because they will tell you something about how well the job was done on the whole.

Last, but absolutely not least, is the question of permits. Did the owner get permits to do this work? A typical basement renovation will require permits for structural changes, electrical, plumbing, and HVAC. If the owner can't produce the permits and inspection reports for each, you should be cautious. If the seller doesn't have permits, call the local inspections department to get them. Some towns have online databases so you can search for permits by the house's street address.

A thermographic-imaging camera can tell a lot about high-moisture areas and heat loss.

MIKE'S TIPS
Beware the "totally renovated" house

I see a lot of bragging in real estate listings about renovations on older homes. You look at the pictures and see claims about all-new electrical and plumbing, everything "totally renovated" — and the house is 80 years old. Now I've got a lot of questions, starting with this: Were permits pulled on all these things — plumbing, electrical, structural? If the owner can't show you permits, you're taking on responsibility for the work possibly having been done wrong. And how much could it cost to repair problems down the road?

There are ways to protect yourself. First of all, ask questions and make sure that you get answers, starting with the permits. Second, pay attention to the finishing details. The great telltale sign that something's wrong is when you see a somewhat sloppy finish. Look at trim and flooring and plasterwork: Do corners meet neatly? Have floors been leveled? Are the seams visible on the drywall? Is there sloppy caulking everywhere?

Anytime there's a visual indication of something that's not good on the surface, just imagine what's underneath it.

 RED FLAGS FOR FINISHED BASEMENTS
- absense of necessary permits and inspection reports
- visible mildew, mold, or dampness
- musty smell
- painted floors or vinyl, carpet, or hardwood directly on concrete. Even if the carpet or hardwood was installed over a vapor barrier of 6-mil plastic, you will see problems in the future.
- wood or metal studs attached directly to exterior walls. Look for areas where you might be able to see how the wall was built: try behind the staircase, in a closet, or where the finished basement leads into a utility (furnace) room, for example.
- new electrical or plumbing: was it properly tied in to existing electrical and plumbing?
- inadequate ventilation for the furnace, if it has been placed in a utility room
- signs of improperly installed heating ducts and air returns in the basement

Now let's get back to what the basement — any basement — can tell us about the house.

STRUCTURAL: BASEMENT WALLS AND INTERNAL SUPPORT

When you were outside the house, you looked at the exterior walls of the foundation and checked for signs of water problems or structural problems. Now, from the inside, you'll look for the same signs, plus a few more. For the most part, our concern is with the exterior walls, since this is where most of the load of the house sits. But, depending on the span (width) of the house, center supports are also needed. Like the foundation walls, those center supports need to rest on deep footings. And don't forget the joists and beams that make up the internal structural components.

BASEMENT WALLS

RED FLAGS FOR BASEMENT WALLS
- walls that buckle, bulge, or lean in any direction. Sometimes you can see a problem from the inside that was invisible from the outside. The amount of movement and the reason for it are the big questions.
- cracks of ¼ inch or more, especially if they run in more than one direction. This probably calls for expert advice.
- visible moisture of any kind — from water trickling through a crack to condensation on walls or windows
- signs of moisture: mildew on drywall (look near floors and corners), insects (which love wet basements), efflorescence (a white crystalline deposit that appears on concrete walls that have been wet). The presence of a dehumidifier also tells you something.
- any new or enlarged window or door. The structure must be supported properly or the new opening will create serious structural problems. Ask to see building permits and inspection approvals.

INTERNAL STRUCTURE

Now for those internal structural components that I mentioned earlier. A lot of people's eyes start to glaze over when the subject turns to joists and columns and beams — those words don't mean a lot to them. But they really are quite simple.

Joists are the wooden boards that stretch from one exterior wall to another — they rest on the foundation walls. When they are topped with plywood, the surface above becomes a floor. Joists have to be very strong to support the floor and all the weight that will rest on it. When they have to stretch too far across an opening, they will start to sag in the middle unless they have some support. That's why we need columns (posts) and beams to create a central support that more joists can attach to. Those columns and beams act sort of like another foundation wall, but in the middle of the basement.

Sometimes there actually is a center wall in the basement, made of wood or masonry, and its purpose is to support the floor joists. Columns (posts) can be made of wood, steel, or masonry (concrete block, brick, or poured concrete). Beams — which also run horizontally, but perpendicular to the joists — are made of wood or steel.

Sometimes — for example, in the case of a very narrow house (less than 18 feet, let's say) — there is no need for any central support, because large enough joists can easily span that space.

Different sizes of joists are used for different jobs. The size of the space determines the size of the joists and the supports needed. These are maximum joist spans: a 2×8 joist can span 12 feet; a 2×10 can span 15 feet, 6 inches; and a 2×12 can span 18 feet, 6 inches. For spans longer than that, more support is needed.

This photo was taken in a basement looking up at the floor joists above. Note the cross-bracing that is meant to keep the joists from moving or twisting. Bracing can also stiffen a floor, reducing how much it bounces when you walk across it.

The joists can also be set closer to or farther apart from each other, within a range. The minimum building code says that joists must be no farther apart than 16 inches on center (which means that you measure from the center of one joist to the center of the next). Setting the joists closer together — at 12 inches, for instance — for a given joist span will make a stronger floor. If manufactured floor joists are used, they can be set further apart, but you are left with a minimum code floor that will still not be strong enough.

 RED FLAGS FOR FLOOR JOISTS AND OTHER INTERNAL STRUCTURAL MEMBERS

- sagging joists. You might see a curve, or bow, to the joists. You might see places where that horizontal length of wood is not fully connecting with the subfloor above it. The other really obvious sign is that the floors above have a visible slope, which is pretty common in older homes. All of these are signs that the floor joists should have been better supported, and that more support may need to be added.

- notches in joists. Sometimes an overly enthusiastic do-it-yourselfer or contractor will cut out a small section of a joist (or several joists), usually to make room for something else: wires, or strapping for a ceiling, for example. Bad idea. Drilling small holes through joists is generally acceptable, as long as they're not at the bottom of the joists, but cutting away the lowest part of the joist weakens it a great deal.

- cracks in joists. Most often these result from notching the wood incorrectly, or sometimes from a knot in the wood itself that weakens the joist.

- places where the joists have been given extra support. The fix might be a good one, or it might not — either way, an added post or another length of wood "sistered" to the original is a sign that others before you have noticed structural problems.

- rotten wood in any structural member. Where there's moisture in the surrounding air, there can be wood rot. The wood becomes spongy and crumbly. When it gets to this stage, it needs to be replaced, or the whole structure will be compromised.

Even if you see lots of these red flags, keep in mind that structural problems can be fixed. In older houses (more than 60 years old), some settling and sloping of floors should be expected.

MIKE'S TIPS
Remedies for sagging joists: More than a facelift

If you move into an older house that has floors that sag toward the middle, you probably need more support in the basement.

Unfortunately, it's not as simple as putting up a couple of posts under those sagging joists and jacking them up until the joists are straight again. You've got to be prepared for what will happen to the plaster and lath in the walls on your main living levels: they're going to crack, crumble, and sometimes come down in chunks. You may also find that doors will no longer fit right, since they've often been modified over the years to accommodate that shifting, sinking floor. That means this solution is best used when you're gutting the house.

To get that floor back where it belongs, you'll first need the advice of a licensed contractor or a structural engineer to determine exactly where the jack posts should be placed for maximum effectiveness. Second, you may need a building permit, because you're dealing with a structural issue. Third, holes will have to be dug to allow minimum 12-inch deep concrete footings to be poured under the posts. Fourth, the jack posts should be set up so that they're in contact with the joists, then raised up until they push the floors above them into a level position.

If you're not gutting the house, you can still use jack posts in the way I've described — but stop when the jack posts are just making contact with the joists. This will give you the support you need without destroying any walls above.

Solid engineered wood beams are a good choice when fixing a sagging floor.

ELECTRICAL

This is not an area that the average person understands very well. In fact, not that many home inspectors understand electrical very well. But I hardly need to say that the electrical system of a home is extremely important for your safety, so there has to be somebody who can evaluate the electrical in any house you're considering. The fact that an outlet has power or a light fixture works doesn't mean it's safe or that it meets code requirements. This is why I believe that every home inspection should at least make available the services of a licensed electrician or electrical contractor.

Let me say more about why a licensed electrician is critical for a thorough home inspection. In older homes where the electrical hasn't been tampered with by renovations and "upgrades," an electrician can judge whether the system is still in good repair, still adequate for the demands of modern life (yours in particular) — and still safe. In older homes that have been extensively renovated, an expert can tell you how well the electrical part of the job was done — and whether it's safe. And in a brand-new home, a licensed electrician can tell you if the wiring shows any signs of being badly done — and whether it's safe.

Yes, even in new homes, safety is a consideration. Remember that in many new home developments, the municipal building inspector does not inspect each and every home. There just aren't enough inspectors to keep up with the pace of construction, no matter how hot or cool the housing market seems to be. The building inspector may examine only a representative number of new houses in a development. That means the house you're looking at may never have been inspected before it was signed off on and declared ready to sell.

Now, when we think about how little is known about electrical systems and how much can be missed in a typical home inspection, it's important to acknowledge that many, many parts of the electrical system remain hidden from view. Most wiring is behind walls. That makes electrical one of the most challenging things to inspect, for a home inspector and even for a licensed electrician. But some aspects are visible, especially in an unfinished basement, and there are always some visual clues that tell us what we might find if we could see through walls.

There are two basic parts to the electrical system in a house. The first is the size of the electrical service —

The electrical box on a home's exterior may indicate the size of the service that goes into the house. The most reliable source for that information, though, is found in the main electrical panel, usually inside the house.

in other words, how much power is available for use in the house? The second is the distribution — how is the power being distributed through the house?

SIZE OF THE SERVICE

Put most simply, the amount of power available to any house depends on how big the wires are that bring in power from the street outside. Incoming power is measured in amps (short for amperes), and it's possible that you'll find anything from 30-amp service at 120 volts to 200-amp service providing 120 and 240 volts. Some people may refer to the voltages in a house as 110 and 220, but for a long time the standardized voltages in North America have been 120 volts and 240 volts.

You hardly ever come across 30-amp, 120 volt service, since it hasn't been used in new homes for decades. That's a good thing, because I don't know anyone who can live on a 30-amp service.

The next level, 60 amps, at 120 and 240 volts, is really not much better. It was common in houses built before the 1960s, and it was fine then, but it can't handle the energy demands of all the appliances, electronics, and air conditioning that most modern families take for granted. Insurance companies sometimes won't cover service at this level or below.

Probably the most common service size now is 100 amps, which is enough for modest sized homes (about 1700 square feet or less if all-electric), or for a larger home (up to 2500 square feet) if space and water heating are gas. For multifamily dwellings or large single-family houses, 200-amp service is needed. Some people also like to have this larger capacity in case they need it in the future.

Keep in mind that service size can be changed, and it's not that expensive in the overall scheme of things. But if it hasn't been upgraded from 30-amp or 60-amp service already, chances are the wiring of the whole house is inadequate and will need work — which can get very pricey.

It's not possible to judge the size of the incoming service just by looking at the cables. We go to the electrical panel, which may be in the basement or utility room, for that information.

The service coming in from the street — whatever its size — runs to a meter socket (or meter base) first. The meter socket may be an integrated part of what's called a service panel, all-in-one, or combined service entrance device, with both the meter socket and the circuit breaker panel in one housing. Service panels are installed on an exterior wall of the house. They're the standard approach to powering a house for areas where full basements aren't common.

In parts of the country where full basements are common, the meter base is usually mounted on the outside wall and then power enters the house and goes through a main disconnect switch, which can be part of the circuit breaker panel or in a separate box just off to the side. Inside this main disconnect switch is either a circuit breaker or fuses. Both act as sort of a safety valve for all that power coming in, shutting off the power if the flow of electricity is greater than the wire and other parts of the system can safely handle.

Some people think that 120 volts is safe to work with. That's dead wrong. There is more than enough voltage at that panel or box to kill a person. Only an electrician should touch that box or try to take the cover off an electrical panel.

Looking at the main fuses or the main circuit breaker is the only reliable way to know the size of the service. In the case of a circuit breaker, the number will be stamped right on the breaker handle. For fuses, they may be in a holder or block which can be pulled out safely. You shouldn't have to open up the panel to or cutoff switch to see the amperage markings.

In the case of fuses, if they're not in a pull-out fuse holder, the cutoff switch cover may have to be opened. This should be done only by someone who knows what he or she is doing — such as a licensed electrician. Once the box or panel is open, the cartridge-like fuses will be visible, and the number written on them indicates the capacity of the service. You may see two 60-amp cartridges — that means the service is 60 amps. If you see two 100-amp cartridges, the service is 100 amps. There's one fuse for each leg or pole of the 240 volt supply.

DISTRIBUTING POWER WITHIN THE HOUSE: WIRING

Over the years, electrical wiring technology has evolved —several different types of electrical wiring became popular and then were replaced by newer, better, or less expensive types in new construction. But many kinds of the older wiring are still in use, and that's a problem today.

Knob-and-tube wiring was the earliest, and a lot of older homes still have this kind of wiring. Installed until about 1945, this system consisted of separate wires (in earlier times, both black, and later, black and white) strung through ceramic insulators called tubes and secured on ceramic knobs.

There was really nothing wrong with knob and tube — in fact, there still isn't anything wrong with it, with four big "ifs." If it hasn't been dam-

Homeowners often attempt to do their own electrical work, which is something I do not recommend. You should always hire a licensed electrician. The use of many different types of wire, including the speaker wire seen here, is a sign of dangerous DIY work.

aged, badly modified, or overloaded, and if it is adequate to supply modern demands.

It's very rare that knob-and-tub wiring hasn't been inadvertently damaged, badly modified or added into, or overloaded. In some houses, all three things have happened. Also, because the original circuits in houses with knob-and-tube weren't designed to meet the demands of modern appliances, they can't supply enough power safely to meet modern demands.

There's another issue with knob-and-tube wiring, and it's a big one. For several years, the National Electrical Code has prohibited the burying of knob-and-tube wiring in thermal insulation. This is because the thermal insulation will trap heat around the wires and cause the insulating covering on the wires to deteriorate. Some insurance companies have set a policy of not insuring houses with knob-and-tube if it's buried in thermal insulation. Most older houses have knob-and-tube wiring in the attic and also have thermal insulation packed around the wiring. Check with your insurance company if the home has knob-and-tube buried in thermal insulation. Aluminum wiring, used for a short time in the late 1960s and early '70s, has other issues. Like knob and tube, it also has a bad name for safety. This is because aluminum wiring don't work well with copper wiring — special methods have to be used to connect aluminum wire to copper wire. Also, the switches and receptacle outlets used with aluminum wiring have to be specially designed and rated to make safe connections. In a lot of cases, as things were replaced, the wrong kind of outlets and switches were used. This can create a serious fire hazard.

The standard these days is copper wiring. It's the easiest for electricians to work with, and it's the best conductor. So why haven't all homes been switched over completely to copper wiring? The answer is that it's expensive for electricians to work behind walls. Wiring a new house is a fairly quick and inexpensive job, sometimes

costing as little as $5,000. Rewiring an older house, where the walls have to remain intact and the electrician has to make as few holes in the plaster or drywall as possible, will start at about $10,000. If you're gutting the house completely and starting from scratch with the wiring, you'll find your cost back down at the low end again.

Back at the panel, you may find some other signs of bad renovation work or handyman specials. If, for example, there are a number of junction boxes near the panel, there are likely more elsewhere in the basement. And junction boxes must always be accessible. Take a look at the cable jacket, too. Are there many different kinds of cable or wire used? That's a sign that many hands have been at work over the years or that someone liked to use scraps. I was in a house once where every color of electrical wire you can imagine was used, which means every gauge of wire too, including speaker wire for lighting. And that home had been inspected and passed with flying colors by a home inspector (not by a building inspector).

When you're looking at an older home where lots of electrical work has been done, you might want the professional advice of a licensed electrician, who can tell you if the wiring is safe and functional. And you'll want to keep in mind that upgrading, and making the house as safe as it truly should be, is a relatively expensive job. However, upgrading will give you peace of mind, not to mention more reliable electrical service, as well as an opportunity to design for what you'll want in the future in terms of electrical, speaker wires, phone lines, etc.

 RED FLAGS FOR ELECTRICAL
- **knob-and-tube wiring that is still live and working. Insurance companies are unlikely to insure houses with any known knob and tube, but they will probably insure you temporarily until you get the wiring replaced.**

- aluminum wiring. No question, a thorough check of every connection by an expert is needed.
- evidence that the electrical has been modified. An electrician needs to assess the quality of the work.
- service smaller than 100 amps, fuses for the branch circuits, or a breaker panel older than 40 years. Some older breaker panels have breakers that do not reliably do their intended job because of poor design or age. Other breaker panels deteriorate due to conditions like high humidity or dust.
- Lights in the house that flicker in sync, or cases where some lights dim and others brighten at the same time. This means a loose connection or damaged wire.
- Wall switches that don't control anything. Sometimes a fixture is removed and the wires from the switch that went to it are not safely capped off.
- hidden junction boxes. Your electrician may be able to spot one — and that's a definite red flag. Any time wires join together in a junction box, the electrical code says the box must be accessible, not hidden behind drywall.
- overloaded fuses or circuit breakers. A licensed electrician needs to judge whether your electrical panel (with fuses or breakers) has been wired properly.
- not enough outlets, or outlets that accept only two-pronged devices. These situations usually happen only in older homes, and they can be a major inconvenience. It can also lead to overloading of circuits.
- outlets near water sources (bathroom, kitchen, laundry room) that are not ground-fault circuit interrupter (GFCI) outlets. A GFCI receptacle is the only safe outlet to have near water, because it will cut off power immediately if there's any leak of electricity out of the circuit. Receptacle outlets located near water sources, or that are outdoors, in an unfinished basement, or a garage should be replaced with GFCIs.
- no permits or inspection reports. Whenever electrical work (other than replacing an existing light fixture, switch, or receptacle), is done on a house, most government building departments require a permit to be taken out and an inspection by a building department inspector to be done. For new construction or remodels, an inspection is typically done before the walls are closed in, and once all the fixtures, switches, and outlets are installed. Ask the homeowner if you can see the permits and the inspection reports.

PLUMBING

Just like electricity, water comes into your house from a municipal source, or if the house is in a rural location, there may be a water well on the property. A pipe connects to the water main on your street, which is why you'll usually find the main water shut-off somewhere close to the front of your house, and most likely in the basement. If you have a water well, a pipe will come into the house from the well.

When we looked just now at the electrical system in a house, we were asking two big questions: Is it safe? And is it adequate?

It's very much the same with water. Is the plumbing system safe — that is, will the water be carried to all points in the house where you want it, without leakage and water damage? Is it adequate — do you have enough water pressure and enough connections to do what you want in that house? In addition to those questions, there is another big one: does the plumbing system safely and adequately get rid of the waste water?

Plumbing is actually very simple. There is water coming in (feed or supply lines) and there is water going out (drain lines). The water comes in through the main line and separates into hot and cold water lines, which run in tandem, a few inches apart, throughout the house to the kitchen, bathrooms, and anywhere else that water is needed. From those same points, waste water is collected in a main vent stack (sometimes called the waste stack or just "the stack") and sent out of the house to the municipal sewer, or to a private septic system if the house is in a rural location.

The rest are details — but important details.

FEED OR SUPPLY LINES

Just as different electrical systems became popular over time, plumbing has a history too. The earliest pipes used for plumbing were made of lead. (In fact, the Romans had a rudimentary system of lead plumbing more than 2,000 years ago.) But lead creates serious health problems in humans, so it was slowly phased out. Today you might still see vent stacks made of lead, but because these handle only waste water, they're not much of a problem.

After lead came galvanized steel and cast iron. The big advantage of galvanized steel was its strength. There were three drawbacks, the first being that it was tricky to work with because each connection had to be made with threaded fittings. The second drawback is that, over time, mineral deposits (scale) build up on the inside, making the inner diameter smaller and smaller — you turn on a tap or the shower and only a trickle of water comes out. The third drawback is that galvanized steel rusts from the inside out until small holes appear in the pipe — and that's when you start seeing real water damage. Galvanized stopped being

installed in new houses during the 1960s. Since it has a lifespan of about 40 or 50 years, some houses still have galvanized plumbing, but it's sure to be near the end of its useful life.

Copper became the standard after galvanized and cast iron. It was easier to work with because a plumber could solder parts together rather than threading them, and copper doesn't react with the minerals in water to create scale buildup. But copper does freeze faster than galvanized, so it has the potential for serious flooding problems, especially if it's installed on an exterior wall without proper insulation around the pipes.

Another alternative is plastic. ABS or PVC plastic tubing has been used for some time now, but in many places the building code allows it to be used only for waste piping, or not at all. This is where a licensed plumber can be really helpful—he can tell you what the code says in your area and he can spot places where the plumbing is not up to code.

 RED FLAGS FOR THE FEED OR SUPPLY LINES

- main supply line made of lead. This means that all your drinking and bathing water will be tainted by lead, which is a serious health hazard. You don't often see it anymore, but if you do, you must think about the cost of replacing it. You can identify lead piping by the large, ball-type connections at the joints and its dull grey color. Plus, it's soft enough so that you can make small indentations if you scrape it with a pocketknife or screwdriver.
- main supply line that is smaller than ¾-inch. Three-quarters is now the standard in new homes (although some are 1 inch or larger). Older homes usually have only ½-inch piping. The size of the supply line will affect

your water pressure. While inspecting the upper floors, check faucets and showers and toilets to see if the water pressure is adequate. Check any basement water sources (laundry sink or bathroom) for pressure as well.

■ sections of copper interspersed with sections of galvanized. Rust can appear at these joints, as the metals react with each other. Sections of copper also indicate that the galvanized is being replaced as it wears out. There is probably lots more galvanized in the house where you can't see it. The first sign that galvanized has broken down and needs repair happens when you get a flood. Other signs are water damage showing on walls and floors just about anywhere in the house. I'll remind you of this point when you're looking through the bathrooms in other parts of the house.

DRAIN LINES

How many stories have I heard from homeowners who are assured by a home inspector that a house is fine, they buy the house — and within days of moving in, they have the drain lines back up on them? Way too many.

Water and waste leave the house by gravity. For this to happen, the lines that take the waste out must satisfy three conditions: they must slope down to allow gravity to work; they must be free of blockages; and the vertical drain lines must not only empty below the house, they must also extend above the roof to allow gases to escape and air to enter the system.

When these conditions are not met, we have problems — sewer gases escaping into the air inside the house, for instance, or water and waste backing up from drains and toilets. These are almost always avoidable if the plumbing is done right in the first place and maintained

properly. The warning signs will always be there.

But it is hard for an untrained person to understand what they're seeing when they look at plumbing, whether it's in the basement or under a sink. This is why I encourage hiring a licensed plumber for this part of any home inspection.

Drain lines are larger than supply lines. They can be made of the same material as the supply lines: lead, cast iron, galvanized steel, or copper. ABS or PVC plastic are also acceptable here; the general rule is that ABS should be used for the stack, while PVC should be used only for in-ground drainage. It's possible that you'll find a combination of materials within one house, since different parts of the plumbing will have been fixed or replaced over time, using whatever type of piping was most popular at that time.

Each fixture (sink, bathtub, or toilet) must have a drain line that takes water, waste, and vapor into the main vent stack. The water and waste go down the stack into the sewer, while the vapor rises up through the top of the vent, above the roof. That same drain line brings air back into the system, which is necessary for proper flushing and draining of water. Testing every toilet and sink in the house is the best way of determining if the drainage and venting has been done properly.

Sewer backups can be caused by an invisible section of the plumbing: the underground part that connects the house waste line to the main sanitary sewer. The waste line under the house may not be large enough for the demands on it. More than likely, though, the line has become blocked or broken. Tree roots, frost, debris entering the system — any of these can cause a problem.

Open up the water sources in the house (which should be done anyway in the course of a good inspection, to test the water pressure) and see if anything backs up. The best way to test for

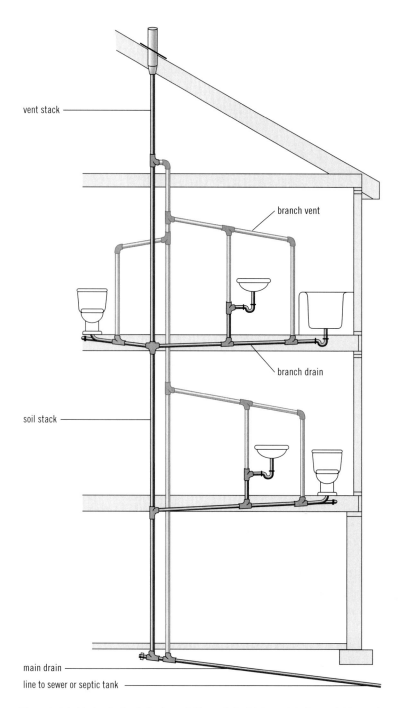

vent stack

branch vent

branch drain

soil stack

main drain
line to sewer or septic tank

We need air behind water for drains to work. The vent stack brings air in from outside your house to push water into the drain. Slow-moving drains might be a sign of a venting problem or drain pipes that are on too shallow an angle.

a drainage problem is to use a camera scope to inspect the waste pipes. Most important, though, you and the home inspector need to observe any signs that water has backed up before, around the drain, or even on the walls if the water/waste level rose high enough. If you see anything suspicious, ask the homeowner if there have been problems, how recently, and what was done about them. You might not get full disclosure, but some information is better than none.

 RED FLAGS FOR DRAIN LINES

- toilets and sinks that drain slowly or gurgle as they drain. There is probably an issue with the venting.
- low water pressure. This is most likely to be a problem at the highest spot in the house, since water pressure decreases with distance from the source.
- the stack isn't high enough. Code requires all vents extend 6 inches above the roof. And in a cold climate, the stack must extend 6 inches above anticipated snow accumulations. If it doesn't, it may become blocked by debris or a heavy snowfall, leaving the plumbing system unventilated.
- residue around the basement floor drain or walls indicating that flooding has been a problem in the past
- if the house was built between 1945 and 1970, or the main drain was replaced during that time, it should be scoped to see if "orangeburg" pipe was used. Orangeburg pipe was very commonly used in the post-war housing boom for underground main drain lines. It's made of wood fibers and asphalt. It breaks down over time and tree roots can penetrate it easily.

MIKE'S TIPS
Rural properties:
Why they're different

No matter how often people hear those funny stories about city folk moving to the country and getting in over their heads, there's always someone else ready to make the leap into the unknown. If you're one of them, make sure you know the following.

Rural properties are different from city properties for a lot of reasons, but probably the biggest have to do with plumbing. First, many rural houses get their clean water from 10' to 200' wells dug somewhere on the property; the water is drawn by a pump into the house as needed. Because it's naturally filtered by the soil, the water is usually clean, but it should be tested for bacteria and other toxins at least once per year (some areas have free testing available from a local health department). The second difference has to do with waste. In the city, waste water from houses is gathered through municipal sewers and treated. In the country, there are no sewers. Each property has its own septic system for collecting waste.

Septic systems come in a variety of shapes and sizes, but the basic premise is the same: there's a holding tank a few feet underground with an overflow opening that allows some water to flow out into the surrounding soil, known as a leach field, which has a matrix of perforated pipes that allow the waste water to seep back into the ground, where it is filtered by the soil. Every few years (depending on the number of people living in the home and the amount of water they use), the tank has to be opened and drained. There are companies that do this kind of work using a tanker truck and a large vacuum-like hose.

Home inspectors can't tell you if a septic system is working properly, or how long it will be before it needs to be cleaned out — or maybe replaced altogether. What an inspector can tell you is whether the toilets are flushing properly and if the sinks and bathtubs are draining well enough. These are signs that everything's in good working order. He should also locate the leach field and determine whether the surrounding soil is wet or smelly. Either could indicate that the field is on its last legs. Replacing a leach field is very expensive.

There's nothing wrong with having a well or a septic system. But if you're looking at a rural property, you're probably going to have to deal with both, and the expenses will be all yours. To prepare yourself, try to get as much information as you can from the current owners. They might be able to tell you how old the well and septic systems are, how well they're working, when the water was last tested, and when the septic tank was last cleaned. Knowing the answers to these questions, you're less likely to be one of those city folk that rural people love to laugh about.

WATER HEATERS — CONVENTIONAL TANKS AND ON-DEMAND SYSTEMS

In some locales, you find a conventional tank-style water heater in the basement that is a rental unit from the local electric or gas company. You'll see a rental sticker on the unit if that's the case. The cost of the rental unit is added to your utility bill. The advantage is that if and when the unit breaks down — and most units have a life span of 10 to 12 years — it will be replaced at no cost to you.

If the unit is not a rental, it comes with the house (listed in the sale). You'll need to examine it for signs of age and deterioration.

 RED FLAGS FOR WATER HEATERS
- rust or leakage at the seams
- no evidence of recent maintenance. Any company that does maintenance will attach a tag or sticker with the date.
- no shut-off valve
- not enough capacity. An average family of four needs at least a 30- or 40-gallon tank.

Plumbing code requires a pressure relief valve (PRV) to prevent the tank from exploding if the heat is not cut off as it should be (from a malfunctioning thermostat, for instance). The PRV should be piped to daylight; if the valve opens, there's going to be a lot of very hot water or steam blowing out the end of the pipe. Also, the outflow of the PRV should be plumbed so that it will drain by gravity. If the PRV leaks, the water should drain away and not be standing in the pipe; the standing water might corrode the valve shut.

In earthquake zones (like much of the Pacific Coast), the water heater should be stoutly strapped to a wall. This is called "seismic strapping," and there's a lot more to it than a length of perforated pipe strap and a couple of nails.

If the water heater is a storage type and is more than five years old, the sacrificial anode, a zinc rod in the tank that corrodes to protect the other components of the tank and plumbing, is probably used up. If there are maintenance records, check as to whether the anode has been replaced.

If you're lucky, what you'll find is an on-demand hot water system. There is no tank in this system, just a unit mounted to the basement wall that is vented directly to the outside. It heats water only as it's needed, so you're not paying for water to be kept hot in the tank all day long. Like conventional units, they can be powered by natural gas, propane, or electricity.

A red flag for on-demand water heaters is a low-quality system. The range of units varies quite a bit, and some can be quite loud when running. Venting requirements vary from manufacturer to manufacturer.

Also, the presence of an on-demand unit doesn't necessarily mean it's the source for hot water. The unit may be used for radiant heating, in which case there may be another hot water supply.

An on-demand hot water system is connected to a manifold for a new generation of plumbing that uses flexible tubes instead of rigid copper pipes.

MIKE'S TIPS
The best time to buy

Statistics show that the most popular time to buy and sell houses is during the warm months of the year — from spring through fall. Most sellers tend to list during these months because they know there will be a bigger group of interested buyers. Buyers often wait till spring to look, knowing that the selection of housing stock will increase as the weather warms up.

When it comes to really knowing what you're getting, however, the best time to look for a house is during the colder months. Why? Because one of the major costs of owning a home is heating it.

When you walk through a home during a January cold snap, you'll get a pretty good idea of where the heating system might not be up to the task. Do your feet feel cold as you walk around in your socks? Cold floors and cold feet usually drive people to turn up the thermostat. If you're in the house for a couple of hours doing an inspection, you can also observe how often the furnace has to run in order to keep the house at a comfortable temperature. If it's running too often, or too long, it's probably struggling and using a lot of energy. Outside the house, you'll also see how well the roof sheds snow and if icicles are building up from the gutters. These are indicators of whether the house has enough insulation, and/ or if the attic is too humid because it's not well enough sealed between attic (a cold zone) and living space (a warm zone).

No matter what time of year you buy, you should request heating bills as proof of the cost to heat the home. Buyers should present these as part of their selling package — along with building permits and inspection reports — but if they don't, you're well within your rights to ask.

HEATING, VENTILATION, AND AIR CONDITIONING (HVAC)

In northern parts of the U.S., heat is one of our biggest expenses. There are lots of older homes with little insulation or none at all, and fuel costs are on the rise everywhere. How efficiently your home is heated, and how comfortably, is going to be a concern when you buy.

The heating system of a house is often grouped with ventilation and air conditioning, because the three are closely related. Their purpose is to provide the kind of air (warm or cool) that's needed at any given time of year, and to make sure that the house and the people who live in it can "breathe" comfortably.

When we talk about heating a house, we're talking about both the fuel that's used to run the heat source (such as natural gas, oil, electricity, or solar) and the way in which the heat is distributed through the house (air moving through ducts, radiators, or electric wiring). There are a lot of combinations that you might encounter while house hunting.

I'm going to take you through some of the possibilities.

FORCED AIR FURNACE

The most common type of furnace available today is forced air. In forced air, or convection, systems, air is heated within the furnace and thenblown through ducts enclosed in the walls or floors of the house to different rooms. Cooled air is brought back to the furnace through separate ducts.

Natural gas is probably the most common fuel, but forced air systems can also be fueled by oil, electricity, propane — even coal or wood. Right off the bat, I'd say that any electric furnace is one to stay away from, or to consider replacing. It's the most costly type of heat you can buy. And oil is at an uncertain stage. Oil prices are through the roof, but bio-fuel may make it more affordable to have an oil furnace. There's still a danger of contamination of the ground under the fuel tank, which can cause very big, very expensive problems.

If the furnace is fueled by oil, there should be a switch that's in the furnace room by the door that's clearly labeled "oil burner cutoff" or similar. This is an emergency shutoff for the fuel oil pump; if there's a leak in the system or some other problem, there has to be a way to shut off the flow of fuel from a safe distance from the burner.

The openings where air comes out into the room are called vents; the other openings are called cold air returns. To avoid hot or cold spots in a house, it's critical that the amount of hot air moving out is equal to the amount of cold air being returned to the furnace. As a general rule, there must be at least one cold air return for each story, and adequate gaps under every door to allow air to flow from room to room. It's preferable for the vents to be located under windows, where the greatest amount of cold air will enter the room, to keep the room evenly heated.

With some forced air systems, you'll find that a humidifier or air purifier has been added, which can be helpful, especially if anyone in your family suffers from allergies. Conversely, a humidifier that adds too much moisture to the house can promote mold growth. For people with severe allergies, some very effective air cleaners/purifiers are available. Central air conditioning systems also tap into forced air systems: in summer they use the same ductwork to move cool air through the house that the furnace uses in winter to move warm air. Other types of air conditioning — such as stand-alone window units or units installed in the attic that have insulated ducts running through the house — are available in houses that don't have forced air systems.

When you see a forced air furnace, you'll want to know if it's a conventional, mid-efficiency, or high-efficiency furnace. Since most conventional furnaces have been phased out by now, you're likely to find either a mid- or high-efficiency furnace.

To illustrate the difference, conventional forced air furnaces would lose quite a lot of heat up the chimney, as well as from maintaining the pilot light, starting up and cooling down, etc. They operate at about 55% to 65% efficiency. Mid-efficiency furnaces claim an efficiency rate of 78% to 82%. High-efficiency furnaces, which have been available since the 1980s, are much more technologically advanced — and therefore more expensive to install. They burn fuel at about 85% to 95% efficiency. Newer furnaces will have a yellow, energy-use sticker on them that will list the unit's efficiency. You may also find an Energy Star label on efficient furnaces.

A hot-air duct runs to a vent in the floor above; the hot air is carried from the furnace through the plenum (the larger, square-edged unit on the right).

RED FLAGS FOR FORCED AIR FURNACES

- furnaces that are at or near the end of their lifespan. Forced air furnaces usually last from 20 to 30 years. You can often see a date of manufacture stamped on the blower unit, which usually indicates the age of the whole furnace.
- excessive noise or vibration. With the furnace on, listen to how it sounds.
- dirt or rust on or inside the furnace. Both are signs that the furnace hasn't been well cared for. Gas furnaces that are regularly cleaned should have tags signed and dated by a licensed gas fitter.
- leaks from the oil tank. This is an environmental hazard that must be taken care of immediately — the cost of not dealing with it can be astronomical.
- old oil tank improperly disposed of. Oil tanks must not be buried on the property — which seems to have been done fairly frequently. The cost to clean up the site afterward is incredible. Think twice about buying if you have any suspicions that an empty oil tank is buried on the property.
- additional sources of heat being used. If you see a space heater being used, it might be telling you something about the effectiveness of the heating system.

RED FLAGS FOR DUCTWORK AND VENTS

- ductwork that is dirty inside. It should be cleaned every year to take care of dust, mites, mouse droppings — whatever can find its way into the ducts.
- ductwork that's been hacked into for additional ducts. Have more ducts been added for an addition to the house? If so, was the furnace replaced at the time of the addition? If not, is it still large enough to service the whole area?
- vents that don't actually have any air blowing through them. While the furnace is running, check every single vent to see that it functions — there have been stories of people who put vent holes in place (complete with register covers) but don't actually connect them to the ductwork.
- rooms that feel colder than others. Do they have enough vents? Do they have any vents at all? What about under the window?

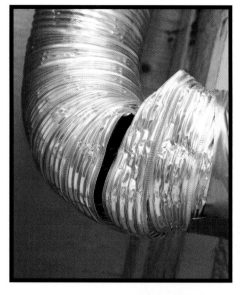

Some red flags for a forced-air system

(Top left) This flexible duct is not a proper duct line and you can see why:
A lot of hot air will be lost because it's split.

(Top right) What exactly is this duct supposed to connect to?

(Bottom left) This heating duct is not connected to anything.

(Bottom right) Cold air returns should be kept free of furniture and carpets.

RED FLAGS FOR CENTRAL AIR CONDITIONING UNITS

- age of the compressor. It is vital to the air-conditioning unit and will last from 10 to 15 years under normal exterior conditions. If it's a water-cooled unit that lives indoors near the furnace, it will probably last longer.
- blown air not cool to the touch. Some systems will take a while to get going, especially if the weather is cold and the system hasn't been on for a few months, but you should still feel noticeably cool air coming out of the vents when the thermostat is set low enough for the air conditioner to turn on. Be careful not to turn on the air conditioner when temperatures outside are very cold, since this could damage the unit.
- if there is no fuse for the circuit breaker to disconnect the A/C compressor, it's a sure sign the unit was installed without a permit

RADIANT HEATING (HOT WATER SYSTEMS)

After forced air, the next most common type of heating system you'll find is radiant heat. In old-fashioned systems there are two parts: the cast iron radiators that I'm sure you've seen in older homes over the years, and the boiler. The boiler will be located in the basement, where it heats water (using gas or oil as a fuel) and sends it through a series of pipes to cast iron radiators located throughout the house.

The great thing about radiant heat is how comfortable it is. Radiators warm the space around them, then the floors, walls, and objects in a room, rather than blowing warm air over them the way convection (forced air) heating does. With the older type of radiators, some parts of the room might stay cool, but the heat is generally pretty comfortable. This can also be among the most efficient sources of heat.

The drawbacks are that the system can't respond quickly to changes in temperatures outside, the cast iron radiators take up a lot of floor space, and there's always the possibility that pipes will burst inside the walls and create a huge mess. Not to mention that you can't connect a humidifier.

If you are interested in a house that is heated in this traditional way, you'll need to bring in an HVAC specialist to really assess the situation. It's worth doing, since many home inspectors won't be able to tell you much about the system, and since replacing any heating system, which may be necessary, is such an expensive undertaking.

RED FLAGS FOR TRADITIONAL HOT WATER RADIANT HEATING

- age of the boilers. They can last for decades, depending on how they were manufactured, but they can't last forever.
- water damage on the floors around the radiators, indicating leaks in the control or bleed valves.

■ a knocking sound, which can sometimes indicate air in the water lines. In any case, the water lines need some attention — they need to be cleaned or flushed annually. During the summer months it's not a good idea to keep water in the lines, since it will simply be standing water for months on end.

Hot water radiators like these are signs of an earlier time, but they're still among the most efficient types of heating. You can tell by the copper pipes and new shut-off valve (left) that repair work has been done here.

RADIANT IN-FLOOR HEATING

This is the newest generation of radiant heating, and I love it. Flexible plastic tubes carrying hot water are embedded in a concrete floor or under ceramic or some types of hardwood. The various tubes are heated through a single manifold, usually in the basement. It's a fantastic source of heat — no dirty ductwork or difficult boilers to contend with, and all the benefits of radiant heat. (It's also possible to get an electric version of in-floor heating, which involves laying down a sort of "electric blanket" under the finish flooring.)

In-floor heating is still relatively new, so you're not likely to see much of it in the average house. Where you're most likely to see it is in bathrooms, where it's becoming almost standard, but whole-house applications are still pretty rare. As with any other system, its success depends on the quality of the product and the skill of the installer. Unfortunately for the home buyer, it can be almost impossible to determine either of those things just by looking at the floor.

 RED FLAGS FOR RADIANT IN-FLOOR HEATING

- damage to flooring from moisture. Some hardwood floors will cup or warp because of in-floor heating; engineered hardwood (not laminate flooring) is the best kind of wood to use because it's entirely stable. If you see water stains on the floor, there probably is (or was) a leak in the tubes carrying the hot water.
- supplementary forms of heat such as space heaters, which may indicate a failure in the system or parts of it.

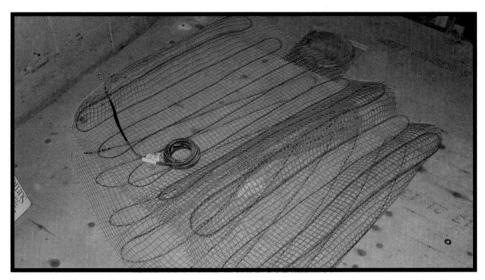

Proper installation of radiant in-floor heating systems may be difficult to determine during a home inspection. In this house, the work was abandoned.

WHAT'S IT GOING TO COST?

If you are considering buying a home that needs some work or if you have big dreams, it's easy to underestimate how much that renovation could cost. Here are some rough cost estimates — the only way to know how much something actually will cost, of course, is to get detailed estimates from reliable contractors.

FINISHING A BASEMENT

Project	Rough Cost Range	Good to Know
renovating, beginning with an unfinished basement	$10,000 and up	A typical basement renovation will require four permits: building, electrical, HVAC, and plumbing.
underpinning (lowering the floor)	$5,000–$100,000	Most building codes require a minimum basement height of 2.1 m (6.9 ft). Some local codes allow for minor variance. A basement bedroom requires — by recent code — a window or door to the outside that's large enough for a person to escape through in case of fire. If you are having the floor lowered, you'll need an engineer to approve plans. Also, do a careful check on the company that will be doing the underpinning — you don't want to mess around here. It has to be done slowly and carefully since you're affecting the structure of the entire house.

ELECTRICAL

Project	Rough Cost Range	Good to Know
upgrading service to 100 or 200 amp, including a new service panel	$2500-$3500	Always use a licensed electrician. You must have a permit for all electrical work.
rewiring the whole house, replacing knob-and-tube wiring	$12,000–$18,000	An electrician will need to cut small holes in walls and ceilings when rewiring the house (unless you are gutting it), so patching and painting will be required too. Rewiring a house is also an opportunity to install wiring for computer networks, sound systems, and more.

PLUMBING AND DRAINS

Project	Rough Cost Range	Good to Know
inspection of drains, help including visual inspection with a camera scope	$250	Inspecting your drains and perforated pipe system may you catch problems early and save you money down the road. It's money well spent.
upgrading main water supply to the house through municipal water service	$1,500–$2,000	Always use a licensed plumber and get permits for changes to the plumbing system.
repairing drainage system to municipal sewers	$1,500 and up	
installing a tankless water heater	$2,000–$4,000 (depending on flow rate)	A tankless water heater is more energy-efficient than conventional water heaters.

HVAC (HEATING, VENTILATION, AND AIR CONDITIONING)

Project	Rough Cost Range	Good to Know
balancing forced-air system with existing ductwork	$300–$500	An HVAC specialist can check and adjust the airflow throughout your house for maximum efficiency and comfort.
installing central air conditioning with no new ductwork required	$1,300–$3,000	
installing a mid-efficiency natural gas furnace	$1,500–$3,000	
installing a high-efficiency natural gas furnace	$2,500–$4,000	The long-term savings of a high-efficiency furnace will usually offset the higher initial cost.

CHAPTER FIVE
The Interior

"My wife and I purchased a small, newly renovated bungalow. I hired a home inspector and used his report to decide to go ahead with the purchase. The home inspector was really not very good and failed to uncover some of the flaws in the home. After living in the home for a couple of years, it became clear to me that the renovations had not been done with permits and were most likely do-it-yourself projects of the previous owner. The new drywall on the first floor had no insulation behind it. My question is: who goes to the trouble of replacing plaster and does not insulate the walls behind? The electrical had hidden junction boxes and connections in the drywall with no boxes. If I ever buy another house that has been renovated, I will ask to see the permits for the project."

—S.R.

Too many people have this attitude about buying a house: "If it looks great, we want it." That scares me.

If there is one message I've tried to get across to people throughout my career as a contractor, it's that you cannot trust how something looks. Fancy finishes, or "lipstick and mascara," as I call them, are not a guarantee that you are buying a good house. Stainless steel appliances, granite countertops, new hardwood or ceramic on the floor — if you make a decision based on features like this, you are buying an illusion.

In fact, I don't care what's on the surface. It's only what's under or behind the surface that matters. If what's there is crap, then you are buying crap, no matter how nice it looks. And it's easy to be fooled.

And that's why, in this chapter about house interiors, I want you to really pay attention. The interior of a house is all about surfaces. Inspecting the interior is all about examining the surfaces and analyzing what's behind them.

If you've come far enough with any house to have an inspection done, I'm going to assume that you've already decided the house has enough bedrooms and bathrooms, that the kitchen is big enough, and so on. What I will tell you is how to determine if they're good enough.

You've already got some clues. By the time you get to the interior stage of the inspection, you've already seen the exterior and the basement. That means you've got some sense of whether the house has major structural or mechanical issues, as well as a pretty good idea about how it's been maintained. Maintenance of the basic structure and mechanicals is usually a good indicator of the level of maintenance you'll find above ground.

MIKE'S TIPS
Deciding what to fix first

A lot of homeowners are in a rush to renovate the kitchen or the bathroom and don't think about what holds their house together and keeps it dry, safe, and standing. With any house — especially one that needs renovations — you should plan your work in the following order of importance:

1. **Focus on safety.** Address any issues that might pose a risk to you, your family, or others who may come to your house. Look closely at steps, handrails, and electrical (especially near sources of water). Get a licensed electrician to help you identify problem areas, and make long-term plans for electrical upgrading, if necessary.

2. **Deal with the structure.** If you see any problems with your foundation shifting or sinking, don't ignore them. They're not going to get better on their own, and they're not going to get cheaper to repair. But they can get worse, and they can cause a whole lot of other problems throughout your house if they're not addressed.

3. **Work from the outside in.** Make sure all exterior systems (roof, gutters, exterior sheathing, and foundation) are in good working order to keep moisture from entering the building envelope. Excavating around your house to seal the foundation properly can cost a fair bit of money, but it's an investment that will dry out that basement once and for all and protect the interior of your house.

4. **Think about fuel efficiency and long-term cost savings:** invest in sealing air leaks, windows, mechanicals, and insulation. Don't throw your money away by keeping an inefficient furnace going year after year; invest in a high-efficiency model that will give you immediate results. Same goes for old windows that are letting in drafts. Replace them with tighter windows, and make sure your installer insulates properly around them. Think about a hot-water-on-demand system and get rid of your water heater. Air leaks are a major cause of high energy bills; they should be taken care of before insulating. Finally, insulate your walls where possible, and make sure your attic is properly sealed and insulated from the rooms below. Otherwise, all that hot air (and your money) will literally go through the roof.

5. **Kitchens and bathrooms, the right way.** Don't settle for cosmetic upgrades. When it's time to renovate a kitchen or bathroom, it's usually time to open up the walls and upgrade plumbing and electrical too. It's more mess and more money than a facelift, but it's worth it for the quality in the end.

6. **Finishes: floors, walls, ceilings, cabinetry, trim.** If your home is dry, solid, and efficient, you can turn your attention to those high-end finishes you've wanted: granite countertops, slate flooring, built-in shelving for the living room — whatever's on your list.

BASIC ISSUES FOR DRY ZONES

You could say that interior living space falls into one of two categories: wet zones and dry zones. Wet zones are the kitchen and bathrooms — places where there is plumbing, where we use water in a controlled way. Dry zones are everywhere else — the living room, dining room, hallways, bedrooms, etc.

Let's look at those dry zones first, because they're probably the easiest to describe. These types of rooms are all pretty much the same from a building materials point of view, so I'll give you some general guidelines that you can apply as you move through different rooms. Our basic concerns are floors, walls and ceilings, windows, doors, stairs, and trim and moldings.

FLOORS

What most people look at when they're checking out floors is, as I've said, how they look. Whether it's a hardwood floor, carpet, vinyl, or ceramic, you want to ask yourself: Is it in good condition? Is it showing signs of wear? If it's hardwood, it can probably be refinished to bring it back to its original condition. Hardwood floors range in thickness from ⅜ to ¾ of an inch, so they can be sanded and refinished many times before they wear out. They should last for decades.

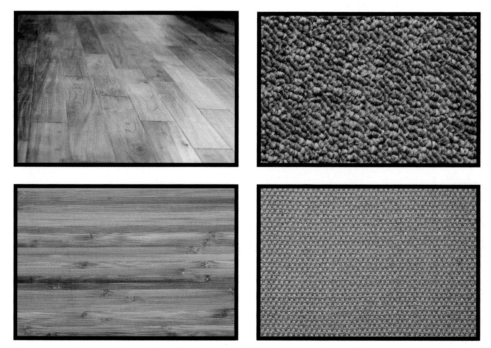

There are many flooring options out there. Hardwood can be refinished, but carpet, once it's worn, can only be replaced.

Unfortunately, you might find yourself looking at a very old hardwood floor that has already been sanded many times. To check the thickness of the flooring, lift the heat registers or cold air return grilles on the floor (if any) so you can see the profile of the floor rather than just its surface.

Carpet and vinyl, on the other hand, have to be replaced if they're wearing out, and it won't be many years before they do. Carpet can be cleaned pretty successfully, but not forever, and it tends to deteriorate unevenly, really showing wear in the high-traffic zones. Vinyl can shrink, and the mastic (glue) that's used to install it has a strong tendency to mold. Ceramic and other types of tile should last for many years if they've been installed properly.

If you're not planning to renovate, or not right away, how the floor looks is a legitimate question. Really, though, the flooring surface should be the least of your concerns. It can eventually be refinished or replaced, and though flooring costs more than pocket change, it isn't going to be the biggest cost you'll ever face as a homeowner. It's what's under the floor that matters: the subfloor, and the joists supporting it.

For hardwood or carpet, a subfloor of ⅝-inch tongue-and-groove plywood over the joists is enough to provide stability, though glued and screwed ¾-inch is better. For any type of tile, the subfloor must be at least ¾-inch tongue-and-groove plywood or oriented strand board (OSB), glued and screwed into the joists underneath. Just as I suggested for checking the thickness of hardwood, you can check the thickness of the sheathing by lifting up a heat register and looking at what's under that top layer of flooring. Cracks in either the tiles or the grout are also a dead giveaway that the subfloor is not up to the job. You might be looking at replacement of the whole thing, sooner rather than later.

Older tile floors may have been laid over a layer of mesh and thinset (mortar that's designed for tiles) applied to a layer of 1-inch wood (not plywood — it wasn't used much until after WWII). That made for a very solid floor, and if you see that type, you're probably looking at tiles that are still in good condition. Problems have come up in more recent years with too many tilers still using mesh and thinset — but a ⅝-inch plywood or OSB subfloor over 2 x 8 floor joists. That just isn't strong enough to stop movement. If you see this combination, you are probably also seeing lots of cracking — or you will.

Under the subfloor are the joists. You already looked at these while you were in the basement, if it was unfinished. Here, in the main rooms, you'll see why those joists are so important. Does the floor bounce at all when you walk over it? Do things rattle on shelves or inside cupboards when you walk past them? If you notice movement like this, there's a problem with the joists. They're not strong enough, either because they're covering too large a span or because they haven't been blocked with enough supports between the joists. Unfortunately, code doesn't require blocking.

Another aspect of the floors is whether they are level. Looking at the foundation has already told you a lot about what to expect. If the foundation is solid, level, and square, there's no reason to expect that the floors will show any signs of unevenness. But if you've seen some problems with the foundation — maybe the roofline sags in the middle, for instance, or the joists you looked at in the basement have dropped down a little from the central beam in the basement — then you should expect to see some obvious sloping of the floors toward the middle.

In older homes, sloping is pretty common, simply because of the way things were built 80 or a 100 years ago. The central posts often weren't supported with substantial footings the way that exterior foundation walls were, so those posts have sunk more than the outside walls, and the floors have followed. That's where the sloping floors come from. But most shifting happens in the first few decades of a house's life, so in old houses you usually won't see the floors sloping any more than they already have.

Sloping toward any of the outside walls is a much more serious problem than a slope to the middle. This indicates that the foundation itself is dropping. If you haven't already noticed a problem from the outside and you see this kind of sloping to one side, you should check out the foundation again in those areas, looking at both the basement and the exterior for clues to what's happening.

Old hardwood floors look beautiful with original high moldings. A small crack between the corner block and baseboard is nothing to be concerned about; it can be filled and repainted easily.

RED FLAGS FOR FLOORS
- surfaces that are low quality or badly worn
- cracks in tiles or grout. The floor is likely not properly supported for tile in either the subfloor or the joists.
- sloping towards exterior walls

WALLS AND CEILINGS

Most of the time you probably don't think much about walls, except maybe for the paint color. You probably think even less about ceilings. When you inspect a house, you need to look beyond color. Color can be changed easily, and it's the cheapest way to improve the looks of a place — or hide things that current owners don't want buyers to see. But what condition are the walls and ceiling? How are they built? What are they hiding? And have they been modified in any way that has compromised the basic structure?

Let's look at the various things you might find.

First, the old standard: plaster and lath. Plaster makes up the inner core of today's drywall. It's mostly a soft mineral called gypsum, and in the past it was blended with water and some fibers such as horsehair to hold it together. Small wooden slats (lath) would be nailed horizontally onto the studs, with small gaps in between the lath, and the plaster would be applied over top. It's a skill and an art to apply plaster perfectly.

There's no need to worry just because you find plaster walls and ceilings. In fact, to many people they're quite desirable because they have historical value and a traditional look. As long as they've been kept dry over the years, they're probably still in fine shape. What you'll often find, though, is that it's difficult to renovate around old plaster-and-lath walls. You have to tear out a fair bit to run new wiring or plumbing, and if you leave the walls in place it's hard to know what you're really working with. Can you find all the old knob-and-tube wiring, for instance? It can be better to open up the wall, run all new wiring and plumbing, insulate, and start fresh with drywall.

If renovations have been done on an old house that you're looking at, you might see evidence that the plaster has been patched, or that it's been replaced with drywall in some areas. If the patching was done by a pro, though, you won't be able to see it at all. You might also find that some rooms of the house have plaster walls while others have drywall. In those cases try to determine if the plaster was pulled down or simply covered up. It will tell you a lot about the care generally taken during the renovations. Covering plaster is easier and faster, but not the right way to do it.

As technologies and techniques changed over the years, builders got rid of the lath and used gypsum board under the plaster. So that's another combination you might see, but not that often.

Nowadays, the standard is drywall. Drywall consists of plaster that has been sandwiched between two layers of paper and made into sheets that measure 4 feet by 8 feet (other sizes are available, but 4×8 is the standard). These sheets are screwed (or sometimes nailed) onto the studs, and the seams are taped and plastered over to make a uniform-looking surface.

Different thicknesses of drywall are used for different applications. There is drywall for bending around corners, drywall for high-impact areas such as playrooms and hallways, drywall for soundproofing, and drywall with a very high fire rating for common areas in commercial buildings. The most commonly used drywall for walls in new homes and renovations is ½-inch; for ceilings, fire blocking, or where the wall studs are more than 16 inches apart, you should be seeing ⅝ inch.

Almost every home now is built with walls of ½-inch regular, paper-backed drywall. It has some fire resistance, it's cheap, it meets minimum code, and — if it is installed properly on studs that have been crowned (installed so the natural curve of all the studs goes in the same direction) and an experienced tradesman has done the taping — you will get a nice finish.

But those are big "ifs." Way too many contractors don't bother to crown the studs, and in new housing especially, nobody gets rid of studs that are warped or twisted (good carpenters would reject these). The framers will use whatever materials have been delivered to the site, even if the wood

MIKE'S TIPS

Tearing up walls can be hazardous to your health

Prior to the late 1970s, a lot of drywall compound (sometimes called mud, and used for filling corners and seams) was made using asbestos. The reason? Fire resistance — it could keep a fire from spreading. But the workers were getting sick — and dying — from a special kind of cancer. Asbestos is no longer allowed in any building materials.

You have to think twice before ripping walls open that were drywalled before about 1980. If you're buying a house that will need a lot of renovations and maybe require new walls, remember that you should have tests done on your walls to determine if there is asbestos in the compound. There are specialists who will come to your house and do this, or you can scrape off small samples and send them to a testing lab. Asbestos is not harmful if it's left in place. But when you disturb it, you will send those dangerous fibers into the air. Don't take the risk.

has sat out in the rain for days or weeks (which is pretty common), and trim off anything that would otherwise jut out and make the wall surface uneven. Later, as the wood dries out, we see a lot of problems with popped screws and uneven walls.

One recent innovation that I like is paperless or mold-resistant drywall. Regular drywall is gypsum covered with paper, but paper is food for mold spores. Paperless drywall handles and looks like regular board but it has no paper, so it can't be damaged by mold. If there is anywhere in the home where mold might have a chance to grow, using paperless drywall is one way to retard its growth. For instance, if you are redoing a basement, your contractor should be recommending paperless drywall there.

Paperless drywall is still not enough for areas with constantly high moisture, like bathrooms. The best choice behind showers, tubs, and sinks is cement board with a waterproof membrane on top. And paperless drywall isn't a solution to a mold problem, so don't accept a home inspector's or contractor's suggestion that it might be. If mold is present, there is a problem with the building envelope somewhere — a gap in the vapor barrier, failed insulation, cracks in the basement wall, etc. — that needs to be found and fixed.

Whether it's plaster or drywall you're looking at, the surface will tell you if there are moisture problems underneath. Look at walls under windows, near floor level, and in corners (and ceilings too) for any signs of mildew. If you see any, you know you've got water coming in behind the walls, and there could be serious mold growth or wood rot going on.

Before we finish up with walls, let's stop for a minute and think about the most important function of walls: structure. For a while now the open-concept look has been the trend. A lot of walls have been taken down to get that look — sometimes the wrong walls.

When you think about doing renovations on a house you own or want to buy, you have to realize that there are structural walls and non-structural walls. Some walls have to be left where they are. Or, if a structural wall (also called a load-bearing wall) is going to be taken out, a steel I-beam or manufactured wood beam has to be properly installed to support the house and carry the load above (including the roof and potential snow loads), transferring it down to the foundation and footings below.

As you go through a home inspection, look for signs that walls have been removed or changed, and ask your home inspector if he thinks it's been done correctly. Look for signs that it hasn't been done correctly — are there cracks in the plaster above windows or doors, for instance? Do the floors sag a lot? This is a real concern if the house is less than about 50 years old. If you have concerns, I recommend that you bring in a structural engineer.

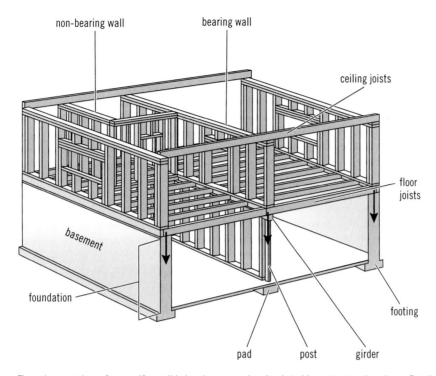

non-bearing wall

bearing wall

ceiling joists

floor joists

basement

foundation

footing

pad   post   girder

The only way to know for sure if a wall is bearing or non-bearing is to hire a structural engineer. But the general rule is that all loads need to be carried continuously down through the structure. If you're looking at an open-concept older home, be sure to ask to see permits and inspections to make sure the structure of the house hasn't been tampered with.

 RED FLAGS FOR STRUCTURAL WALLS
- unusually large rooms for old houses
- unusual seams on ceilings and unusual patches in floors
- floors that slope in some rooms but not others
- mismatched trim work on doors and baseboards

 RED FLAGS FOR WALLS AND CEILINGS
- mildew and/or water stains. There has been moisture. The source of the moisture has to be found and fixed.
- patch jobs on plaster. Whoever did the work didn't have the skill to do it right.
- cracking or crumbling plaster. Some cracks are just the result of age and the natural settling of the house. Others indicate real structural problems.
- uneven or wavy drywall or popped drywall nails. The studs were probably not crowned in the same direction, and/or they weren't evened out before the drywall was installed.

■ visible drywall seams. A good taper will apply three coats of plaster over every drywall seam, with each layer spreading wider and fanning out for a smooth and totally invisible finish. If you can see the seams, the taper wasn't a pro.

WINDOWS

The possibilities for windows are almost endless. They vary in style, insulating value, watertightness — and the quality of their installation. When you're inspecting windows, you need to be aware of all these factors.

If we're speaking really generally, there are five main types of modern windows: double-hung, single-hung, casements, horizontal sliders, and fixed. A double-hung window has two sections, and both of them move up and down. A single-hung window looks the same but the top section is fixed, so only the bottom section can be moved up and down. A lot of people love double-hung windows because they're the most traditional-looking (especially with dividers in them), and because both sections of newer double-hungs will open inwards, so they're very easy to clean.

Casement windows, with awning windows above, bring lots of light and air into the house.

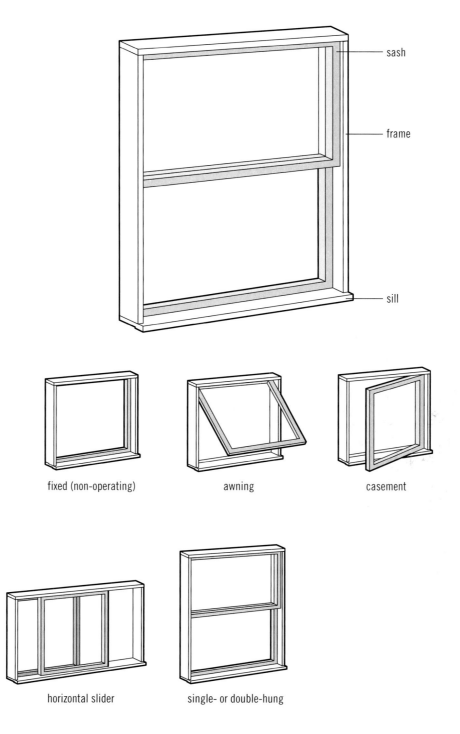

sash

frame

sill

fixed (non-operating)　　　awning　　　casement

horizontal slider　　　single- or double-hung

Casements are tall windows hinged on the side or top and bottom so they will pivot open, usually with a mechanism at the base of the window. An awning window is similar, but it is horizontal and hinged at the top; the sash is also opened with a mechanism at the base of the window. With horizontal slider windows, either one or both sashes will be moveable, but since they don't have any mechanical parts, they're much cheaper than any other type of window. They're often paired with a fixed window above. Fixed windows don't open at all; they're just panes of glass. The most common type of fixed window is a "picture" window. You could also call glass blocks a type of fixed window.

Unless you're in the group that wants to buy a completely restored older home, with all the original details preserved or brought back, you'll probably do best by looking for vinyl windows. They're easier to clean and will last longer than metal, and they don't promote heat loss the way metal does. Wood-framed windows can be beautiful, but they require continual maintenance.

The biggest issues with windows, by far, are heat loss and moisture. All windows lose heat. Double- or triple-paned windows, which have thermal glass or argon between the panes, will help to minimize the loss, but they can't eliminate it.

A common mistake when replacing windows is not leaving enough space to allow for expansion of the materials. A tight fit may stop the window from opening and closing properly.

How well the window has been installed will make all the difference in keeping heat where it belongs and keeping moisture on the outside. If your home inspector has a thermographic imaging camera, this is an area where it will come in handy: he can check for variations in heat and cold around the window, which will tell him if it's been well insulated. Failing that, there's always the tissue trick: you can hold up a tissue around the window and see if the tissue moves because of drafts. Of course, on a day without wind, you probably won't see any movement anyway.

Moisture always lets you know it's there. Look carefully around every window for signs of mildew and bubbling or peeling paint. The window sill could be affected, as well as the wall below.

If you're seeing condensation on the windows during an inspection, you're looking at one of five possible causes:

1. The seal between the two layers of glass has been broken, and warm air is meeting cold.
2. The windows haven't been properly installed or insulated. Cold air is getting in and meeting the warm air inside.
3. If the house is new (two years or less), the wood-framing members likely got wet during construction and are still letting off moisture.
4. The house is so well sealed that it's actually too airtight. Not having enough air movement will cause condensation.
5. The house could have a problem with the HVAC (heating, ventilation, and air conditioning), which means a heating specialist would need to be called in.

In an old house (left), water has caused some damage to the window frame and sill. Even in a new house (right), condensation is beginning to cause problems.

RED FLAGS FOR WINDOWS

- signs of water damage or wood rot on the window frame or the wall below it. Condensation is a problem or rainwater is getting in. It could be an ongoing problem, and more serious water damage could be hiding behind the wall.
- non-functioning windows that won't stay up without a support or that won't lift up at all. Some older windows have been painted shut over the years. With newer windows that won't lift, the problem is likely improper installation.
- cracked glass
- missing screens
- drafts around the window frame when the window is closed. Not enough insulation was used during installation — or maybe none.
- too many windows for the heating system. This is a concern with additions especially. Ask an HVAC specialist if the system is up to the job.
- low-quality windows. You're looking for at least two panels of glass, and solid hardware and mechanicals.
- old single-pane wood windows without storm windows. This will be a drain on your heat. Wood windows also require more maintenance than vinyl, so check the condition of the putty that seals the window, and the condition of the paint on the frame.

DOORS

Interior doors vary in style and quality almost as much as windows do. Hanging a door the right way and installing the handset (the knob and strike plate) takes the skill of a good finish carpenter. With new construction, pre-hung doors should make badly fitting doors a thing of the past, but it's still important to check. Far too often I have seen them installed badly.

In older homes, where door frames were built and fitted on site, the skill of the installer was even more important. Shifting and settling in older homes would cause doors to stick, or keep them from closing at all. The "solution" was often to trim or shave the door at the top or bottom.

For an old or new door, the most important things to look at are quality and function. Is it solid rather than hollow-core? Does it swing properly and close properly?

Any door to the exterior, or to an attached garage, should be solid (either wood or — my preference — metal with a polyurethane or hard foam interior) and fire-rated, with all gaps well sealed against weather and gases. If there's no porch or small roof to protect the door from the outside, there should at least be a storm door to keep rain and snow outside, where they belong.

RED FLAGS FOR DOORS

- doors that won't shut easily, or at all
- doors that scrape the floor,
- cheap, hollow-core doors
- exterior doors not protected from the elements by a roof of some kind or by a storm door
- no weatherstripping around exterior doors.

STAIRS

I've seen some stair work by contractors that just made me shake my head. Stairs are supposed to be safe. But they're complicated enough that they're easy for an amateur to mess up, in new construction or in a renovation. In really old houses that haven't been kept up, they can become unsafe. Imagine how easy it will be for someone to fall and get hurt if stairs and railings aren't built right and maintained right.

Stairs should be wide enough to use easily, with enough height clearance (at least 6 feet, 8 inches, at today's minimum code) for almost anyone to walk without worrying about their head. The depth of the treads should be comfortable (at least 10 inches), and the same is true of the height (rise) of each step (no more than 7 ¾ inches according to code, preferably 7 to 7½ inches high). Each step must be an equal height from the top to the bottom of the stairway. If you notice that you're tripping over the stairs, it's a sign that something isn't right. Code allows for a ⅜-inch variation in riser and tread dimensions, but that's not the right way to build stairs.

Stairs need to be structurally correct in order to be safe. You might not be able to see the support, but you might be able to tell if it's not there. Look for gaps anywhere in the staircase, or where the stringer (the long piece of wood that the steps fit into) attaches to the wall. Feel for too much bounce.

The handrail should feel solid when you grip it and be at least 34 to 38 inches high, by minimum code. Spindles or balusters (the pieces that support the handrail) should always be vertical — horizontal members of any kind are not allowed by code for the simple reason that they're a climbing hazard. They just aren't safe for kids to be around. Spindles should be less than 4 inches apart — again, it's a safety issue.

RED FLAGS FOR STAIRS

- visible gaps between the stringer and wall
- steps that are too steep for safety
- treads that are too narrow (not deep enough) to step on comfortably
- no handrail, or a handrail that's shaky or too low
- horizontal supports under the handrail, or vertical spindles that allow the passage of a 4-inch sphere

TRIM AND MOLDINGS

Trim and moldings — which include door and window trim, baseboards, and crown moldings — are not structurally important. They're important for two reasons: how they look, and what they tell you about the people who built or renovated the house.

Some contractors, and some handymen, don't even think about the fact that all trim should be consistent. If it's an old house with 8-inch or 12-inch baseboards and you're redoing the master bedroom, it's going to look out of place to use 3-inch baseboards. You've got to respect the history of the house.

Even worse is trim that's been done sloppily. When trim is done right, baseboards meet perfectly on outside corners and mitered crown moldings meet perfectly on inside corners where wall and ceiling come together. If any pieces of trim have had to be joined together to form a continuous section, the line should be pretty much invisible: the cuts should be angled to fit together rather than made at 90 degrees. End cuts should have been painted or stained to match the rest of the trim, and a thin bead of caulking used to seal gaps between trim and walls. If you see that all these have been done correctly, you know that a good finish carpenter worked on that house.

One red flag for trim and moldings is sloppy finishing, including gaps and unpainted end cuts. These tell you that whoever worked on the house didn't know what he was doing, or didn't really care.

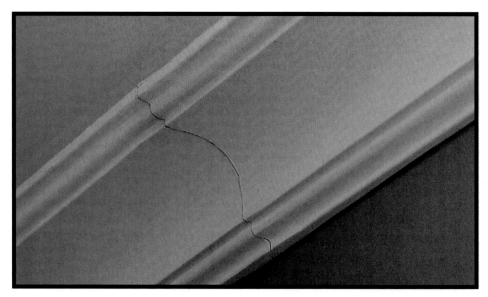

I'd rather not see even a hairline crack like this on crown molding or other trim. Professionals fill in small gaps before putting on a final coat of paint. Remember: Anytime you see a visual indication of something that's not good, just imagine what's underneath it.

BASIC ISSUES FOR WET ZONES (KITCHENS AND BATHROOMS)

Kitchens and bathrooms take a lot of wear and tear, so chances are you will have to do a kitchen and/or bathroom renovation at some point in your life. There are a few major questions to ask as you're buying: how old is the room that you're looking at, how well was it built or renovated, and how long will it last?

If a kitchen or bathroom is newly renovated (within the last two or three years, let's say), you can be sure that the owners are looking for a return on their investment. You need to judge the quality of that renovation carefully. If it's a much older kitchen or bathroom, you'll probably need to invest in a renovation yourself.

Either way, kitchens and baths are among the most expensive areas of any house, especially in an era when people want showcase kitchens and spa-like bathrooms, not just places to cook and get ready in the morning. Just because you see a new bathroom or kitchen, don't assume that there's nothing to worry about. There are still too many people who approach renovations with a "fast and cheap" mentality (which equals crap, every time), and too many contractors who take shortcuts to finish the job faster. You need to look for quality, not just shiny new surfaces.

THE KITCHEN

There are so many aspects to examine in a kitchen. Is the layout good? There should be a good work triangle, with the three main appliances (refrigerator, sink, and range) easily accessible to each other. Is there enough workspace and adequate storage, with quality countertops and cabinets? What about plumbing, ventilation, and lighting? Are appliances included, or will you have to buy new ones?

Cabinets

The most important and expensive part of any kitchen is the cabinetry. On the surface, you won't be able to see much difference between good and bad cabinets — at least not when they're new. Underneath, I have seen some of the worst crap imaginable being sold for criminal prices. If you know a little about cabinets, you'll have an easier time separating the good from the bad.

In cabinetmaking, the biggest drop in quality over the years has been with the boxes behind the doors (known as the carcase). If you're looking at a house from the 1960s or earlier, you'll probably find cabinets made from ½-inch to ¾-inch plywood — incredibly strong and durable and probably overbuilt. As material costs rose and new products like particle board, melamine, and MDF came along and lower grades of plywood were produced, the

MIKE'S TIPS
Five things you need to know about layout and design

Some things that are called design are really a matter of taste. Others aren't. Here are some guidelines about what good design looks like (or doesn't).

1. Every room needs a window, unless it's an interior bathroom. In that case, a fan that vents to the outside is required by code.

2. Kitchens should be built around a work triangle of sink, refrigerator, and range. Single-wall galley kitchens should be a last resort.

3. Bedrooms are private spaces: you should never have to cross through one to get to another room.

4. An enclosed entry (sometimes called a vestibule) is worth looking for and worth investing in, for two reasons: you'll stop cold air from getting into your living space, and you'll have a place to put all the stuff that goes with real life (boots, coats, umbrellas, etc.).

5. A bathroom should not open directly into the kitchen or a main living area. The entrance to any bathroom needs to be sheltered by a privacy zone such as a small stretch of hallway.

A work triangle of sink, refrigerator, and range is the core of a well designed kitchen.

carcase became the obvious place for manufacturers to save money. Newer cabinets aren't likely to be made from durable stuff.

Look for thicker materials — at least ⅝ inch for the top, bottom, and sides. Typically the carcase is made from some core (plywood, particleboard, or MDF) covered with a thin veneer of wood or melamine. I'd say about 90% of the kitchens installed today are melamine veneer, so chances are that's what you're going to be looking at.

What matters with any carcase is how it is constructed. Butt-jointed, glued, and stapled melamine carcases are the lowest of the low. The glue doesn't stick to melamine, so only the staples are holding the carcase together. A carcase like that will fall apart eventually.

The joints should be rabbeted so that the glue comes into contact with raw particleboard on both pieces and provides structural strength. And forget the staples. Particleboard doesn't hold screws very well, let alone staples. The best way to connect the sides is with wooden or steel dowels. The wood dowels, when glued, provide tons of mechanical connection. The steel dowels rely on themselves to make a strong connection. You want doweled carcase sides if you've got a melamine carcase.

Cabinet backs are often made from ⅛-inch Masonite, but I would only accept ½-inch as a minimum. More important, they should be fastened with glue and dowels into a channel cut into the sides into the back of the cabinet, not surface-mounted. The back plays a big part in stabilizing the whole cabinet. Staples and glue are okay here, but there have to be plenty of staples. It has to be very firm, with no flex at all.

Drawer cabinets should have additional stretchers (horizontal pieces of solid wood that stabilize the two sides of the cabinet) in the carcase between the drawers. Sometimes there are none, or they are just at the top and bottom.

The quality of drawer slides varies a lot. You get what you pay for. The best slides are designed to be installed under the drawer. Side sliders, which are cheaper, are mostly fine. Some slider systems use plastic drawers, where the only part that is wood is the drawer face. I think they're just ugly.

The best wood drawers are ¾-inch ply or solid wood with the back let into the sides, not butt-jointed. The drawer bottom should be ¼-inch-thick plywood and slid into grooves along the sides, not stuck on the bottom of them. Dovetail joints are the very best. Any time dowels, biscuits, or finger-joint corners are used to connect the components, you are looking at a well-made drawer.

Cabinet doors come in all kinds of materials. Solid wood is the best. MDF (not my favorite) is often used, but it's the finish that really matters. The cheapest are thermofused. That's an MDF door that has a PVC film heated and vacuum-molded onto the face of the door. Next is oil-based paint. Both are cheap and the finishes don't last. The best reasonably priced finish is a high-quality catalyzed lacquer. The top of the line is a polyvinyl finish. It looks great and lasts forever.

Even the best-quality cabinets can look like garbage if they aren't properly installed. Look at how the cabinets are connected to the wall. They have to be level. Your doors and drawers should open easily without touching or rubbing against anything else. Make sure filler strips are used in between cabinets when needed — that's essential. If it doesn't look right, more than likely it isn't.

 RED FLAGS FOR CABINETS
- low-quality cabinet carcases. Thin, flimsy materials won't stand up over time.
- low-quality cabinet door finishes. Look for solid wood, wood veneer, lacquered, or polyvinyl finishes. Thermofused or painted cabinets will wear badly, and you might already be seeing this.
- cabinets that are badly installed. They should be level and square, with doors and drawers perfectly in line with each other. Doors and drawers should open easily without touching anything else. There shouldn't be any visible gaps between cabinets if the proper filler strips have been used.
- cheap hinges. The quality of the hinges might suggest the quality of the cabinet carcases and doors. Good hinges suggest good quality all around.
- on older cabinets, any signs of moisture damage such as rotted wood, especially under and around the sink

Counters

In countertops, granite has been king for a while now. It's a prestige product, even though it's becoming more common all the time, especially in new construction. I find that a granite countertop is often used as a carrot to get people interested in a new development or a flipped house, so you have to look carefully at the quality of everything else around it. How detailed and well done are the edges? Has it been built up with bullnosing to be at least ¾ inch? Look carefully at the cabinetry finishes. Don't let a slab of granite fool you into thinking the whole house is top-notch.

At the same level as granite — in terms of both price and perception of value — are slate, marble, and any other type of natural stone. All these natural stones, as well as concrete (which is increasingly popular, though I'm not sure why) need to be sealed regularly, or their natural porosity will

With imagination, skillful design, and professional installation, stock kitchen cabinets can give you a custom look. Many cabinetry companies also manufacture coordinating units that can be used in living and dining rooms.

make them prone to staining and gathering bacteria. Solid-surface products such as Corian or quartz composite are also very popular and don't need to be sealed. Stainless steel is the most non-porous and easy-to-clean surface you can find, but you see it less often for residential kitchen countertops. Any of these counters have been purchased at a fairly high price.

In the less expensive category are tiled counters and laminates. I have issues with tiled counters because the grout between the tiles can allow moisture to penetrate through to the plywood substrate. And, unless epoxy grout is used (one of the few places I recommend it), the grout will absorb whatever comes in contact with it: you'll be looking at food and beverage stains, and a lot of bacteria. Laminate countertops are still the most common type you'll see, because they're just so much more affordable than any other kind. Of course, they're prone to chipping, burning, and other damage.

 RED FLAGS FOR COUNTERS
- gaps between seams or damage such as chips and cracks on laminate counters. Where there are cracks, the laminate often gets wet too, which will cause problems over time.
- stains on natural stone counters. These are a sign that the sealer hasn't been maintained.
- inadequate counter space, especially next to the sink or range
- water damage. Look at the underside of the kitchen counter near the sink. When sink rims haven't been properly sealed, counters get saturated and begin to rot.
- Not enough electrical circuits serving the kitchen counters. Current code requires at least two 20-amp circuits serving the kitchen counters, another 20 amps for the dishwasher and disposal, and another circuit (either 15 or 20 amps) for the range vent hood.

Floors

 RED FLAGS FOR KITCHEN FLOORS
- slope or uneven level, too much bounce, or cracks in tile grout. Check the support in the subfloor.
- broken tiles. This can happen because there isn't enough subfloor support, or it can be the result of something mechanical — like a heavy pot being dropped on it.
- worn vinyl or linoleum. It may be near the end of its useful life.
- layers of flooring. I always recommend going back to the subfloor. Adding layers just masks problems and can even create new ones, such as cracked tiles.

Kitchen sink options are endless —
if you're willing to spend the money.
Customized cutting boards and drain
racks make kitchen work easier
(above). Undermounted sinks are
gaining in popularity (left).

Plumbing and appliances

Appliances (range, refrigerator, dishwasher, microwave) may not be included with the house you're looking at, but often they are. Take a look at the listing to see if they're mentioned; if not, they're probably mentioned under exclusions. If they are included, you need to ask for manuals, warranties, and proof of age, but just observing them will also tell you a lot. If there isn't a dishwasher, will you want to install one, and is there room for one fairly close to the sink (and the water source)?

For sinks and faucets, you're looking at both function and quality. Keep in mind that even these everyday features come in a range of styles, quality, and price. A light-gauge stainless steel sink is going to cost a whole lot less than a top-of-the-line apron-front porcelain sink.

Turn on the tap and watch how quickly the water drains away. Look under the sink for signs of leakage or water damage from earlier leaks. Take note of any musty smells — it could be mold. Make sure the faucet operates easily, without leaking.

If you've brought a licensed plumber in for an inspection, have him check out the plumbing under the sink for anything that's unusual or not to code.

Even if a bathroom fixture is new, always turn on all taps and showerheads to check water pressure.

RED FLAGS FOR PLUMBING AND APPLIANCES
- appliances (if included) that are nearing the end of their lifespan and will have to be replaced soon
- slow drainage
- leakage, signs of previous water damage, or a musty smell
- unsafe outlets. Any outlet within 6 feet of a water source must have a GFCI.

This plumbing is wrong (for one thing, the trap is missing), which is a sign that other plumbing in the house may not be up to code.

Lighting and ventilation

A kitchen needs lots of choice when it comes to lighting. Overhead lighting, ambient lighting, task lighting over the sink, range, and workspaces — all of these are important if you want to enjoy working in the kitchen.

The work we do in kitchens releases enormous amounts of moisture into the air every day. If we don't want moisture problems in our home, we have to keep moving that moisture outside. Windows are the most basic form of ventilation, but fans — quality fans that are powerful enough to draw air out — are also needed in kitchens.

 RED FLAGS FOR VENTILATION

- no window and/or no fan, or a fan that doesn't vent outside. A common problem in DIY flips or quick renovationss is a range hood that vents nowhere, or into the wall cavity, the garage, or another room. It must vent directly outside or it will cause condensation and moisture problems. Turn on the fan and check to see where it exhausts.
- fan not powerful enough to remove moist air. Test the fan by holding a paper towel up to it: if the paper towel drops away, the fan isn't strong enough to do any good.
- a recirculating fan rather than a fan that vents directly outside. Charcoal filter fans claim to be as efficient as direct-vented ones, but think about it: you're not trying to clean the air (that's what the filters on your furnace do), you're trying to get cooking moisture (and toxic fumes, in the case of gas or propane stoves) out of the house.

Range hoods start with the cheapest $35 model and go right up to top-of-the-line stainless steel ones. The real questions are how well does the range hood exhaust moist air from the cooking zone, and is it vented outside?

10 things to know about mold

1. Mold is a variety of microscopic organisms that require two things for growth: a food source and moisture. When both of these are present, mold will start to grow fairly quickly and will keep reproducing.

2. Mold grows if there is too much moisture in the house for one reason or another. The most common reason is that water is entering the structure because something is failing: the roof, the exterior sheathing, the windows or doors. Another reason might be that a lot of moisture is being produced in the house and there is not enough ventilation to remove it. If you're seeing mold anywhere in a house during a home inspection, you need to ask the inspector what might be causing it and how serious the problem is.

3. Your health is at risk if there is mold in your house. Small amounts usually don't cause much of a problem, but the larger the area of mold, the more likely that you or someone in your family will have an allergic reaction to its toxins. Pregnant women, infants, the elderly, and people with weakened respiratory systems are especially at risk.

4. Discoloration is often a sign of mold, but not all discoloration indicates mold. Soot from candles, chemical residue from cigarettes, outdoor pollution entering the home—all these can cause discoloration that has nothing to do with mold. Mold can be just about any color. Dab just a drop of bleach onto a suspected spot: if the spot loses its color or disappears, it might be mold. If it doesn't change, it probably isn't. (Use bleach for testing only.)

5. There are hundreds of different kinds of mold that might grow in a home. You can pay to have someone do an air test that will tell you if there are mold spores in the air and how high the concentration is, but it's often not necessary. If you think what you're seeing is mold, it probably is. Why waste your money to prove what you already know? Use the money to deal with the problem.

6. Mold can usually be cleaned, but it will reappear if the source of the moisture is not addressed. Building materials such as plywood and OSB can often be cleaned pretty well, but others—such as drywall—can't.

7. If the affected area is relatively small (a few patches, less than a square yard each), a healthy person can usually clean it safely, if he or she uses mild cleaners and takes precautions, such as wearing gloves and a good dust mask. Bleach should never be used to clean mold, since it is toxic enough to cause reactions too. If the area is extensive (larger than a sheet of plywood—4" x 8"), you should have specialists to do the removal. Whenever mold has to be cleaned away, the next step is just as important: finding and dealing with the source of the moisture.

8. If you suspect there is mold behind a wall, be very careful about what you do next. Hitting damp, moldy walls with a hammer is not a good idea, since you'll just spread the mold spores into the air, making the situation worse. If the spore concentration is high enough, the spores could even end up in the duct work and spread throughout the home when the furnace or air conditioner is running.

9. If you need to call in specialists, make sure you use a contractor who is a licensed mold abatement specialist and has adequate insurance to do this kind of work. Anyone else will only make the problem worse. A competent real estate agent or home inspector should be able to recommend a mold abatement company.

10. The best solution for mold is prevention. Watch the building "envelope" for any signs of water penetration, and deal with them quickly. In high-moisture areas such as bathrooms and kitchens, use products that will minimize the food that lets mold grow (concrete board rather than drywall under any wall tiles, for instance). Throughout your house, and especially in high-moisture areas, make sure there is adequate ventilation to get that moist air out.

BATHROOMS

If you go into a bathroom and it doesn't smell right, it usually isn't right. I'm talking about that musty, mildewy smell that comes from water that never dries completely and causes deterioration in the walls, floors, etc. Even in quite new bathrooms, water will cause damage very quickly, damage that you can see and smell. And then, of course, there's that other smell that will tell you of possible sanitary drain problems.

There can be a lot of reasons why this happens, from careless bathroom use to lack of ventilation to outright failure of the building materials themselves. Let me explain those reasons a little more. The first one — carelessness — is fairly obvious.

The second — lack of ventilation — is a really important one in a bathroom. By minimum code, every bathroom requires at least a window or a fan to move moist air out of the room. I prefer to see both. Unfortunately, the type of fan that minimum code allows in a bathroom (50 cubic feet per minute (cfm) for switched fans and 20 cfm for fans that are always switched on) isn't actually strong enough to do much good. People think they're ventilating their bathroom because they have the fan on, but the air is just being spun around. Just as you did in the kitchen, check the bathroom fan by holding a paper towel or piece of toilet paper up to it while it's running. Does it stick or does it fall down? There's your answer. Again, as you did in the kitchen, check to see that the fan actually exhausts to the outside, rather than into the wall cavity or some other room.

The last reason why you might be smelling or seeing mildew or mold has to do with the materials used to build the bathroom, and how they were installed. So many products are good products — until someone installs them

Holding a tissue up to the back of a running fan will tell you if it works well. If it doesn't stick, there isn't adequate suction power.

in the wrong place or uses the wrong method. Take caulking, for example. Latex caulking has lots of uses, but bathroom use is not one of them. It will support the growth of mold. Only a silicone caulking should be used in a wet area.

On the other hand, some products are doomed to fail, always. The best example is green wallboard. Years ago it was seen as the best drywall to use behind tile in a bathtub or shower area because it was "moisture resistant." It's still listed as acceptable by minimum code, which is incredible when you consider its failure rate. I think it deserves the award for most useless product in the industry. A small upgrade to cement board as a tile backer will extend the life of a bathroom by many years, but many contractors — maybe because they want to save their customers money, or maybe because they just don't know any better — are still "economizing" with green wallboard behind tiles.

Unfortunately, you can't tell just by looking at tiles whether they have green wallboard behind them or cement board — the wallboard will be completely covered up. But there are ways to determine how bad the damage is from bathroom moisture. First of all, use your nose.

Second, look for mildew and water stains everywhere: around every corner of the tub and shower (including the places where they meet the floor), on

A deep soaking tub is a popular feature in many newly renovated bathrooms. Before putting one in, though, you need to ensure that the structure of the house can support the full tub's weight.

the ceiling, and under the sink (both in the cabinet and under the counter, and around the base if it's a pedestal sink).

Third, feel for softness. Most materials in a bathroom are meant to have a hard surface: tile, flooring, walls. If you feel sponginess in the flooring or behind bathtub tiles, you could be looking at a problem. (Don't press too hard: something could give way, and it's not your house yet.) Are any tiles loose, cracked, or missing?

What else are we looking for in bathrooms? Water pressure and proper drainage. Turn the faucets full on to determine whether the water pressure is adequate. In older houses, where the water lines leading into the house from the municipal source tend to be smaller in diameter than today's standard, it's not uncommon to find fairly low water pressure. But water pressure problems can also come from improper plumbing.

Maybe the toilet is too far from the main vent stack, or the waste line that runs from the toilet to the stack is set at too shallow an angle. There could be similar problems with the shower or bathtub drainage. Watch how quickly the water drains out of the tub when you turn on the shower for a few minutes. If it drains slowly, it could be clogged, or there could be a

A more common bathroom sight: mildew near the top of the shower stall. When there isn't enough ventilation and not much room overhead for air movement, mildew is inevitable.

More and more houses are including luxury features, so I'm often asked about saunas and steam rooms. Unless they're in separate buildings, away from the envelope of the main dwelling, I'm not in favor of them.

Why not? Because they create more moisture than most houses can stand, and our building practices haven't caught up yet. There are so many special considerations for building a sauna or steam room the right way — but I've hardly ever seen it done right. I believe that in a few years, we'll be seeing a massive breakdown of these "spas" inside people's homes and terrible problems with moisture and mold.

Many home inspectors list spas (including saunas and steam rooms) among the things they won't inspect, and I don't blame them. At the moment, there's almost no way of giving them a clean bill of health.

plumbing problem. A licensed plumber is the best judge of whether everything has been done right.

If there's a newly updated bathroom, you need to ask what exactly was done. Did they move walls, and did they move plumbing? If they did, structural and plumbing permits are required. Ask to see those permits and inspection records. If they don't have them, that worries me.

Finally, you want to consider bathroom storage. Is there enough? Even beautiful bathrooms will look terrible if there's nowhere to put all the stuff that you use every day. What you need for a powder room will be different, of course, from what you need for the main family bathroom or master bathroom.

 RED FLAGS FOR BATHROOMS
- musty, mildewy smell
- no window and/or fan, a fan that doesn't draw enough air out, or a fan that doesn't exhaust directly to the outside
- visible signs of moisture damage: mildew or mold in the tub or shower area, under the sink, or on floors
- soft, spongy feel on the floor or tiled surfaces
- slow, sluggish toilet flush and/or tub drainage
- inadequate storage

THE ATTIC—COLD ZONE OR WARM ZONE?

The attic is the last part of the interior you need to inspect. What you're looking for will depend on whether the attic is a cold zone (which is the normal use for attics) or a warm zone (living space).

Let me explain what I mean. Many people get confused when I say that an attic is a cold zone. Don't we want the inside of our house to be warm? Well, yes — but not everywhere.

Until people started to renovate attic space to make it into living space, the attic always served as a buffer between the warm living areas of the house and the outdoors. We use a vapor barrier and insulation on the attic floor to keep warm, moist air from escaping into the attic. Warm air will always move up, especially if there is cold air — from a cold basement, for instance — to push it. The attic should have plenty of ventilation (remember those roof, ridge, gable, and soffit vents I talked about earlier) to keep the air at the same temperature as the outdoors. That keeps your roof healthy and free from the condensation that causes wood and shingles to rot.

These days, however, many people have turned attics in older homes into living spaces. That means the attic has moved from being a cold zone to a warm zone, and now we've introduced some extra challenges and potential problems along with the extra space.

Converting attic space in a home is impossible without a major renovation, since almost every new home is built with a system of roof trusses that takes up all the available space above the roofline. None of those trusses can be removed without compromising the entire structure.

Let's look at the different issues you need to know about, depending on how the attic is used.

IF THE ATTIC IS A COLD ZONE

For an attic to function properly as a cold zone, three things are critical: ventilation, vapor barrier, and insulation.

When we looked at the exterior of the house, we did a preliminary assessment of the roof ventilation by looking for how many vents there were. I prefer to see gable vents, soffit vents, and roof vents, especially long ridge vents. Now, when you go up into the attic with the home inspector, you'll be able to see how well that ventilation is functioning.

(Is there access to the attic? If there isn't, that's a serious problem: the building code requires access if the attic is more than 30 square feet in size and is more than 3 feet high.)

Look first of all to see that the vents are open, not blocked. Ideally, soffit vents will have baffles (long, rigid plastic vents) that direct air from the outside into the attic, up over the insulation, and out through the roof vents. You should be able to see daylight through the soffit vents — this will tell you that they're not blocked by insulation. Ideally there will be one soffit vent for every four bays (a bay is the space between a pair of rafters).

Good ventilation, along with a proper vapor barrier and adequate insulation, will mean that you feel and smell fresh air in the attic, not mildew, mold, and rot. Insulation should be dry, not damp at all. If it's below zero when you're inspecting the attic, the roof sheathing above your head should be free from frost. Frost will develop only if cold air in the attic has met warm air rising up from the living space below and created condensation.

Vapor barriers in the attic need to be continuous and well sealed. They should be installed on the warm side of the insulation — next to the attic floor (actually the ceiling of the room below). Some insulation batts have a facing that acts as a vapor barrier; they should be installed with the facing towards the occupied part of the house, not toward the attic.

There are lots of areas where air can leak into the attic, such as around the attic hatch, plumbing stacks, and ceiling light fixtures that enter the attic. These should all be sealed off to prevent warm air from flowing up. A good clue for air leaks is dirty insulation in certain areas—that shows you have air movement, which isn't good.

 RED FLAGS FOR COLD-ZONE ATTICS
- no attic access
- damp insulation. When fiberglass or loose fill insulation gets wet, its insulating value is drastically reduced.
- not enough insulation. Attics require from R-25 to R-40 across the entire attic floor.
- frost on the roof sheathing above
- visible condensation, mildew, or rotted wood
- dirty insulation
- no sign of soffit vents or baffles

IF THE ATTIC IS A WARM ZONE

Once an attic space is finished, the cold zone has been lost, or reduced to a matter of inches (the space between the finished ceiling and the roof above it). That poses some challenges for insulation, vapor barrier, and ventilation.

But before I go into that, it's important to realize that attic conversions are complicated, because this is space that, once again, was never intended as living space. They have to be done by someone who's knowledgeable. Turning an attic into a living space may require changes to the roof (possibly), electrical (likely), and structure (absolutely). Again, permits are important here. Can the owners produce both building permits and inspection reports? If they can't, how will you know if the work has been done right? If there are no permits, run.

One of the key things in an attic is the floor. Many old attics have "floors" that are built of 2×4s. That means they were designed to support the ceiling below it and to act as structural support for the roof, but not as a floor for walking on. They have to be beefed up to at least 2×8. If you don't have a building inspection report, it will be difficult to know what's under the finish flooring. The same is true of the stairs to the attic, if they aren't original to the house: are they supported properly?

What about ductwork to the attic? Depending on the size of the space, you may need more than one register for warm air and one cold return. (Remember that these always work in tandem, for heat balancing.) Now, the ductwork may have been added correctly (you'll want to check every register while the furnace is turned on), but was the extra demand on the furnace taken into account? Was the furnace upgraded? This is always a concern when we add to our living space, whether in the attic or through an addition to the house.

Many people put skylights in a finished attic or they enlarge an existing window. In both cases, this is structural. Have the windows been properly framed and installed? Is there a permit and an inspection report?

To go back to my first comment about losing our cold zone when the attic is converted, you have to consider insulation, ventilation, and protecting the roof from moisture. When you finish an attic, you're essentially creating a cathedral ceiling, with a very small space between the roof and the finished ceiling — not enough space for insulation and proper air flow.

Building inspectors look at the structure as it's being built or renovated, and they also check the insulation and vapor barrier before the walls are closed in. If it's been inspected, you have at least some assurance that it's been done right. But I don't even like building code recommendations for cathedral ceilings: there just isn't enough room for the air flow above the insulation. I prefer to see 2 inches of high-density polyurethane spray-foam insulation. It's got the highest R-value of any insulation, and it doesn't need any other air flow or any additional vapor barrier.

The makers of asphalt shingles will say, of course, that insulating this way is bad for their shingles because it doesn't allow the roof decking and shingles to breathe. That's probably true, but there are ways around it. For one, another roof layer can be built on top of the existing one, with strapping that will create that breathable zone under the roof deck. A better solution is to move to a steel roof, which also requires strapping over the existing roof deck but which is a material that won't melt with high temperatures. Sometimes the solution is a different product.

A red flag for warm-zone attics is no building permit or inspection report. You will have very little proof that the attic conversion has been done safely and to minimum code.

Attics cannot be easily converted into additional living spaces. Ceiling joists are typically engineered to support the ceiling and are usually not strong enough for a floor above, which has to support considerably more weight. In this house, a contractor cut out the bottom of the roof trusses and replaced them with other beams (top). This caused serious structural damage to the roof and required a major repair.

MIKE'S TIPS
Insulation basics

In a finished house, there aren't a lot of opportunities to see what's behind the walls. But aside from those behind-the-wall electrical and plumbing concerns, there is one issue that you need to be aware of: insulation. An unfinished attic is probably the best place for a home inspector to get a sense of how much insulation is in the home. That's because the walls are not closed in with drywall and the floor joists are exposed. Here are a few things to know about insulation.

1. An unfinished attic requires some form of insulation to keep the heat of the house from escaping into the attic in the winter. The most important factor is sealing off — as tightly as possible — the attic from the living space below it. What we want is to create a thermal break between those two zones — that is, to keep the warm air of the main house from coming into contact with the cold air of the attic. The reason, of course, is that condensation forms when hot meets cold, and moisture is the enemy of just about every building material we use.

2. There are many types of insulation, but all of them are measured in R-value, which rates the material's resistance to the movement of heat. The higher the R-value, the better the material insulates. By code, an attic requires from R-25 to R-40 across the entire floor.

3. Even if a material has a high R-value, its effectiveness can be greatly reduced if there is a lot of air loss. This means that insulated walls (or attic floors) have to be protected against drafts. Minimum code requires a vapor barrier on the warm side of the insulation to stop air movement. But a vapor barrier can be compromised by seams that aren't taped properly, not to mention nail holes or recessed lights in the ceiling (in attic insulation).

Mineral wool batts (right) have good
insulating value for walls and excellent
fire resistance. Pink rigid-foam insulation,
sometimes called extruded polystyrene (previous
page), is one of the best insulation types for basement
walls and floors, since it provides a full thermal break
between cold gound and warm air.

4. The types of insulation you're most likely
to see during a home inspection are these:
fiberglass batts or blankets (often pink or yellow);
mineral wool batts; blown cellulose fibers (recycled,
shredded, and chemically treated paper); extruded
polystyrene (rigid-foam insulation); and polyurethane
spray foam insulation. Only the last one has the advantage
of creating a complete thermal break in the attic, because it
gets into every crack and crevice.

5. Unless your home inspector has a thermographic imaging camera, it will be difficult to know if the walls of the house are insulated.
With the camera, he can see variations in temperature even behind the
walls. When walls are well insulated, there will be very little difference
in temperature between exterior walls and interior walls; the insulation will
be stopping the heat from moving out or in.

WHAT'S IT GOING TO COST?

If you are considering a home that needs some work or if you have big dreams, it's easy to underestimate how much that renovation could cost. Here are some rough cost estimates — the only way to know how much something will actually cost, of course, is to get detailed estimates from reliable contractors.

KITCHEN RENOVATION

Project	Rough Cost Range	Good to Know
typical renovation with good-quality pre-fabricated cabinets, , countertops and tiles	$10,000–$20,000	A typical kitchen renovation will require at least two permits: electrical and plumbing. It may also require a structural permit.
luxury renovation with custom cabinets, high-end tiles and countertops	The sky's the limit.	Don't be tempted by a quick-fix solution for your kitchen renovation. You probably need to gut the kitchen to make sure it's done right. Not all "custom" cabinets are custom-made. Real custom cabinets are built to order, which takes time. You need to allow 6 to 12 weeks. In my opinion, it's worth the wait because these cabinets are stronger and built to last. Plan your lighting carefully and give yourself options. Think about ambient lighting, as well as functional task lighting under the kitchen cabinets, above the sink, and above islands. When shopping for countertops, think about how porous the material is. Granite and other stone surfaces have to be sealed regularly.

BATHROOM RENOVATION

Project	Rough Cost Range	Good to Know
typical renovation with good-quality fixtures and tiles	$10,000–$15,000	A typical bathroom renovation could require at least three permits: structural, electrical, and plumbing.
luxury renovation with top-quality fixtures and tiles	The sky's the limit.	Don't be tempted by a quick-fix solution for your bathroom renovation. You probably need to gut the bathroom to make sure it's done right. Invest in a high-quality ventilation fan and make sure it vents outside. Proper ventilation in a bathroom is the best way to fight moisture and mold. Don't use green drywall in the bathroom, even though building code allows it. Use concrete board in the tub and shower area and mold-resistant drywall in the rest of the room. If you are thinking of moving a tub or putting in a larger one (like a soaker tub), make sure the structure underneath it can support the load.

WINDOWS

Project	Rough Cost Range	Good to Know
replacing all windows	$10,000 and up	Vinyl windows are a good low-maintenance choice.
installing bay or bow windows	$2,500–$5,000 (depending on size of construction, insulation required, etc.)	Adding a bay, bow, or a larger window will affect the structure of your house. You will need a permit, and you must ensure that it's done right.
installing a skylight	$750–$2,000	Proper installation of skylights is a must and requires a flashing kit to prevent leaks.

CHAPTER SIX
Holmes Inspections:
Four Case Studies

Case Study #1
The Flip: A Total Cover-up

If I had done a home inspection for these people when they were first looking at this house, I would have told them to run like hell.

Case Study #2
Eyes Wide Open

I always say that anything is possible in a renovation—anything. When I went to inspect this midtown Toronto house, I found a young couple who believed that too.

Case Study #3
New House, Same Old Story: Minimum Code Sucks

Think you can avoid problems by buying new? Think again.

Case Study #4
Making It Right on a Century Home

When you're thinking of buying an older home, what are the most important things to look for? What if you want to maintain an older home properly?

So far in this book, we've looked at the areas of a house you need to know something about before you move ahead with a home inspection. I've explained a lot, and identified some of the red-flag areas you need to watch out for. But there's nothing like real situations to make it all make sense.

In this chapter, I've used case studies to show you what a home inspection might look like in four real-life situations. I chose these four houses because they demonstrate some of the scenarios you're most likely to encounter — a house that was renovated and "flipped" for a quick profit, an old fixer-upper with problems galore, a new house with issues of its own, and a beautiful older home that's been pretty well maintained and professionally updated over the years. Each of these houses has something to show you.

What you'll see in the following pages, of course, are only the highlights of the extensive inspections we did on each one of these homes. When you hire a home inspector to look at your own home, or to advise you on a house you're interested in buying, you'll be looking not only at the highlights but at every last detail. A good home inspector will draw your attention to everything, and he'll explain it to you — or, if he can't explain it, he'll advise you to bring in a licensed professional to give you expert advice.

Case Study #1
The Flip: A Total Cover-up

If I had done a home inspection for these people when they were first looking at this house, I would have told them to run like hell.

You might describe the house as a cute little three-bedroom bungalow with a bonus two-bedroom apartment in the basement. But that's where we have to draw a line between what something looks like and what it really is. Because what is this house really? It's a total cover-up — total. A quick flip and quick cash for the seller has meant a world of pain for the buyers.

The nicest thing you can say about whoever did this work is that maybe they were trying their best but just didn't know what they were doing. The worst thing you can say is that they knew exactly what they were doing but were trying to make a quick buck, so they cut corners and didn't care who got suckered along the way. Somehow or other, the home inspector who went through this house gave it a pretty clean bill of health.

A young couple bought this house — their first house — because it looked good. There was a nice skylight in the living room, some great-looking new hardwood on the main floor, new kitchen cupboards, granite counters, stainless steel appliances, air conditioning — lots of perks. The apartment in the basement was attractive to the couple because the woman wanted to have her mother live with them, but in a self-contained unit. And the exterior was totally new: new roof, new front and back porches.

That's what this couple thought they were getting.

They got an idea of what they'd really bought, and how big their problems were, as soon as they moved in. It was January, and the gutters were leaking so badly that every day a sheet of ice would build up on the driveway, making it almost impossible to get to the side entrance to the apartment. The owners realized that the back part of the house was almost completely uninsulated—it had once been a back porch, and the previous owners must have closed it in quickly without properly finishing it for year-round living.

Inside, of course, those back floors and rooms were freezing. There was no heat source in the main bathroom, every closet was unfinished, and the owners began noticing bad smells in the laundry area of the basement.

When warmer weather took care of some of the problems, others appeared. The new asphalt parking pad was so soft that the owners' barbecue sank into it — almost to the top of its wheels. And in the basement apartment, the tile grout became discolored and water was seeping up through the laminate flooring.

What I found during a site visit were safety issues, heat-loss issues, moisture issues, plumbing and electrical issues — all the result of shoddy workmanship. Take a close look at what I discovered.

IMPROPERLY INSTALLED EXTERIOR STUCCO

What the inspection report said: "Generally acceptable"

The product used here on the exterior is extruded foam covered in a thin layer of stucco. This stuff comes in sections like building blocks, so it's relatively easy to install, and it's fire-rated for safety.

But it does require proper wrapping of the house first, using a house wrap — not plastic, like I found here — and the stucco has to cover the under-side of the foam as well. Here, the foam is exposed on the bottom, and it's already starting to break off. Because it's not protected, it's going to draw moisture up into it and the stucco and foam will break apart in no time. Give it a year or two and it's finished.

We can also see that the foam and stucco was simply installed over whatever the previous exterior was. It was probably siding, judging by other houses around here; most of the time people do not cover brick. The real giveaway is when you look up at the soffits: they're really narrow — only about 3 inches — because whoever installed the stucco just ran the stuff right over the previous siding and up under the soffits. They should have taken the soffits and siding off, run the stucco up to the roof, then fitted new soffits on. They probably saved time and money, but it still looks bad and it's completely wrong.

Now the good thing is that there's a nice thermal break. However, if they did insulation with a vapor barrier in the inside of the home, a trap has been created. So, with a thermal break on the outside and a vapor barrier on the

inside, moisture has now been trapped. And when you trap moisture, what happens? Mold.

GAP WHERE MOLDING DOES NOT EXTEND FULL LENGTH OF FASCIA

What the inspection report said: No comment

The finishing of the fascia is so bad that it's visible even from the street, but the home inspector didn't even make a note of it. In fact, the home-owner asked the inspector if it was okay and was told that it was "fine." It's nowhere near fine. If we can see behind that metal, then water and snow can get in behind it — trust me. It's an issue.

SKYLIGHT INSTALLED WITHOUT FLASHING

What the inspection report said: "Generally acceptable; check caulking and flashing at junction with roof annually"

This is not how we install skylights. I'll tell you right now, whoever installed that skylight cut into the roof right through the shingles, installed the skylight, and then caulked around it. There should be a flashing kit designed for skylights that runs under the shingles and up along every side of the skylight to completely seal out the water. I guarantee that this skylight will leak before too long. The inspection report says the flashing should be checked annually, but there isn't any flashing to check, let alone to keep the water from coming in. And that caulking can't do it all.

EAVES AND DOWNSPOUT DETERIORATING BADLY

What the inspection report said: "Rectify/repair"

Well, at least the inspector caught this problem: these gutters are ready to give way. If they aren't replaced before too long, the owners could have water backing up under the roof and into their attic space — not what they really want to deal with. And the plastic downspout should never have frozen (it runs vertically, not horizontally, so the water shouldn't build up in it), but it's the cheapest product on the market.

WRONG LIGHTS, WRONG TILES

What the inspection report said: No comment

On the outside, a bunch of pot lights have been stuck in the soffit. But there's not even enough room for them to be installed here, because of that narrow soffit, and these lights are not meant for outdoor use. Same thing for the granite on the front steps. Granite should never be used outside because it gets way too slippery. The way they've done it — by just going over the old steps, and by using grout instead of caulking at the edges — is going to let rain in; the rain will even seep in under the door. And because there's really nothing to cover or protect that front door, the rain will get in and start to damage that new hardwood inside. In fact, I can see that it already has. This is really shoddy work.

DANGEROUS GAS METER LOCATION

What the inspection report said: "Caulk around exhaust outlet covers"

Caulking around this exhaust outlet is the least of my worries: that laundry exhaust outlet is right next to the gas meter. And on the other side of the meter is the central air-conditioning unit. Local gas company standards state that nothing is allowed within 5 feet of the gas meter — and 6 feet is a better rule. We make that allowance so that if the gas regulator ever leaks — which it will, because it's designed to let off gas — none of the gas can ever come back into the house. Here, with the laundry vent so close by, the gas meter is perfectly placed to send gases right back into the house — not a safe situation at all.

ASPHALT SHINGLES ON A FLAT ROOF— A MAJOR PROBLEM

What the inspection report said: "Generally acceptable"

You never use shingles of any kind on a flat roof. Period. To use shingles, code requires a minimum roof slope, or pitch, of 2 in 12 (and I prefer to see 4 in 12), to allow for drainage. We don't have that minimum here. No doubt about it, these shingles are going to leak and that's going to cause moisture damage to the roof decking below them — not to mention causing the problems inside the house. The inspection report didn't even make a note of this flat roof on the back of the house — it stated that the whole house has a peaked roof, which isn't true.

A BACK PORCH THAT'S NOWHERE NEAR MINIMUM CODE

What the inspection report said: "Generally acceptable"

Everything on the back of this house is made of the cheapest product available. This porch was built with spruce, which is indoor lumber — you don't want to use spruce on the outside because it warps right away, as this is already doing. You need to use cedar or pressure-treated wood. Not only is this the wrong material, the porch is also built in a way that goes specifically against the building code: you cannot build railings with horizontal members, because kids can climb up them — they must be vertical. And it's nowhere near high enough: 36 inches is the minimum height. Nothing I see here would pass a building code inspection.

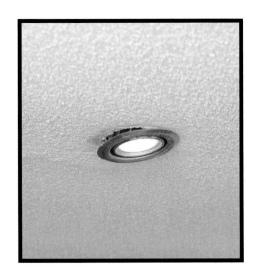

POT LIGHTS INCORRECTLY INSTALLED AND LEAKING HEAT INTO THE ATTIC

What the inspection report said: "Generally acceptable"

I never allow recessed lights in the top level of a house. The heat from those lights — which extend into the attic space above them — will go up into your attic, adding to the heat that's already trapped there. This roof has two layers of shingles and I didn't see any kind of exhaust up there — no roof vent or anything like that — so is the heat getting out? The answer is no.

To help prevent condensation, we want to stop the heat from escaping into the attic. A pot light that goes up into an attic should be a canister designated at AT, which stands for air-tight. The AT canisters are gasketed, which creates a vapor barrier to stop heat loss from inside. These recessed lights look like puck lights, which are cheaper versions meant for under cabinets. They're not even meant for ceilings.

POOR OR MISSING INSULATION

What the inspection report said: No comment

This infrared thermographic imaging camera shows images using different colors to tell me about the temperature of different sources. Today it's quite warm outside, and a laser point on the wall tells me it's 81.3 degrees Farenheit here, so the room is very hot — the wall is holding the heat. We can tell that these exterior walls have very little insulation in them, if any.

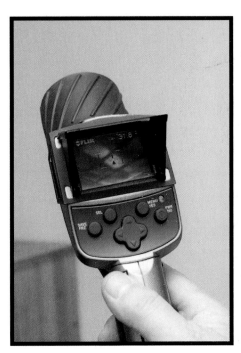

MISSING DUCTWORK IN WALL

What the inspection report said: No comment

I can see the studs by using the thermographic imaging camera. As I move the camera around, I see quite a bit of cool air from the air conditioner escaping up into the wall — it's just being lost in the wall cavity. That's a waste of cool air and energy. There should be rigid ductwork running up to the register, sealed off so that hot or cool air isn't lost in the wall cavity.

ACCESSIBLE DRIP REQUIRED ON VALVE

What the inspection report said: "Rectify/repair water shut-off for south exterior water faucet"

The inspector caught this minor problem. This is the outside faucet, which is located within the wall. It's supposed to be shut off for the winter because it's not a tap that can stay on in below-zero temperatures. You can get galvanized fittings that go through the wall, and you can leave them on, but this isn't one of them.

I don't see a drip, or water-release valve. When you shut the water off, you've got to open up the tap to allow water in the pipe to get out so it doesn't freeze in there. You've got to have total access to it. This is a minor repair, but it needs to be addressed.

INCORRECT DRYWALL INSTALLATION AROUND TOILET

What the inspection report said: No comment

They've actually drywalled over the existing wall and drywalled the toilet right in. You can't get at the toilet to fix it or clean it. Another sign that these "renovators" did not know what they were doing.

OVERLOADED CIRCUITS AND POSSIBLE HIDDEN JUNCTION POINTS

What the inspection report said: "Generally acceptable"

The panel looks pretty good, but when I see all the electrical in this house and then see so many empty spots left on the panel, that tells me a lot of the circuits are overloaded. I know that they did not use the total capacity of this panel; instead, they tied in the electrical at many different spots in the home.

That tells me there are hidden junction boxes everywhere, and that's totally illegal. A junction is an box with a plate on it, often where a light or some other electrical service used to be. Here they've tied wires into the junctions. By minimum code, junction points must be accessible, because that enables you to tell how many things have been tapped into it. If ever a common line goes down because of a loose ponytail or wirenut, you can get to it and solve that problem without punching a million holes in your house.

PLUMBING AND WIRING STAPLED TO STUDS

What the inspection report said: No comment

There's a newly built studded wall here in the furnace room. None of the plumbing or wiring along this wall is within the studding; it's stapled to the outside of the studs.

Whoever did the plumbing was not a licensed plumber. Whoever did the electrical was not a licensed electrician. Whoever did the work was not even close to trained.

EMERGENCY SITUATION: POSSIBLE GAS ESCAPING INTO THE HOUSE
What the inspection report said: All heating and cooling and electrical systems were "generally acceptable"

The gas water heater is a concern because of how it's been vented. An HVAC specialist must be called right away because there are issues of gas escaping into this home.

WET BASEMENT FLOORS

What the inspection report said: "Generally acceptable"

We can actually see the subfloor — the structure — under the laminate wood flooring. Just by pushing on the floor you can see the water coming out. The wood has absorbed so much water it can't absorb any more, so it's moving it up through the floor. There's also moisture building up under the ceramic tile section of the floor.

The source of the water? Maybe it's a foundation issue. Maybe it's the plumbing going up to the kitchen sink. Again, specialists should be brought in to evaluate everything.

The flooring is now a massive problem. Everything from the wood structure down here must go. All that wood is now soaking wet. I can only imagine that there is mold galore. If you have more than 10 square feet of mold, you have to bring in a mold removal team. The percentage of mold in this home right now is very high.

The bottom line? I'd guess it would cost a minimum of $150,000 to fix everything. And that's a minimum. The people who "renovated" this house not only covered up all the old problems, they introduced a ton more.

The worst of it is that you couldn't sell this house to anyone — not if you wanted to sleep at night. What a stressful situation for this young couple!

IS THERE ANYTHING WRONG WITH FLIPPING HOUSES?

Your opinion of flipping probably depends on which side of the transaction you're on.

To people who are buying, fixing up, and reselling real estate, flipping is just good business. They love the thrill of the hunt for that underpriced diamond in the rough, the transformation — and the profits, of course.

But if you end up buying a house like this, you're more likely to think that flipping is a con game.

In fairness to people who like to play the house-flipping game — and there are more of them all the time — I don't think most of them are trying to rip anyone off. They are trying to maximize the amount they can make by turning that property over quickly, which often means making some decisions that are not going to benefit the house, or the next buyer. They resort to what I call "lipstick and mascara" — cover-ups that look good but that are not going to last.

IF YOU'RE THINKING OF FLIPPING . . .

If you're renovating with an eye to selling, make sure you aren't just covering up problems. Take care of the basics like plumbing, electrical, HVAC, and insulation, but do it right — hire professionals. Make the house better than it was when you bought it. Then, once you've done that, make it look good.

Not every renovation you do on your house will give you the same return on investment if you're doing it to sell. You might replace your roof and windows and fix the foundation — and that's the right thing to do. Practical renovations are smart and the best to invest in for the long term.

Unfortunately, a lot of homebuyers don't get that excited about these very important points — but a new granite countertop and stainless appliances will impress them every time.

Generally speaking, kitchen and bathroom improvements give you the best return on your investment. They increase the value of your house more than most other renovations. Creating additional space in the house, through a basement renovation, is another good place to put your renovating dollars, but remember that it takes a lot more than some drywall, paint, and carpet to do these things right.

Keep in mind that financing an extra house, or even financing the renovations, can be a pretty heavy burden to carry, even for a short time. You need to educate yourself before you try anything like this, because flipping is not as easy as the home shows make it look.

Always remember: if you are renovating to sell, get permits, use quality materials, and hire skilled professional people to do the job right.

IF YOU'RE BUYING . . .

There are two basic ways to tell if the house you're looking at is a flip. The first is the sales record. The second is in the details of the house.

When you're buying, the sales record of the house is really important to ask about. Your real estate agent will be able to get you a total sales history for any house you look at — when it sold recently, and for how much. This is useful information because it lets you know how much the house has appreciated in value — or whether the current owners are just looking to cash in on a hot real estate market by inflating the asking price.

If a house is a flip, that sales record is even more important. Most flips are done in less than a year, so if the last sale was only a few months prior to the current listing, chances are you're looking at a flip. Aside from sudden emergencies, there's really almost no other reason to own a house for such a short period of time. In the case of a flip, often no one even lived in the house during that time: the owner just went to work in there or brought in different contractors, then listed the house again as quickly as possible. (This can be another tip-off: is the house empty when it's listed, after a short period of ownership?)

Some people will move into a home they're intending to flip. In cases like this, they're more likely to spend at least a year in the house, since one year is the minimum length of time you can own a house in the U.S., if you want to avoid paying short-term capital gains tax on the profit of your sale (which can be as high as 35%): in U.S. law, your principal residence (the home you live in) is sheltered from capital gains tax, but only if you live in it for two years out of the last five years. Some people make a living (or supplement their income) by moving from house to house, year after year, "fixing them up" as they go and making a nice profit each time.

I said there is a second way to tell if you're looking at a flip — and a bad flip at that. That way is to look closely at the details in a house. There are always signs that someone has tried to do a fast-and-dirty reno to get the house looking fancy and get a big return on it.

RED FLAGS FOR FLIPS

1. New everything

Unless they have a lot of money, most normal people don't renovate the entire house while they're going about their everyday lives. A house is usually a work in progress, so there will be some things that are freshly done and others that are less new. Yes, there are very house-proud people out there, and most people these days know they have to make their place look clean and polished before the buyers see it, but most of the time a house still looks at least somewhat lived-in. A flipped house, however, looks perfect — or does it?

2. Empty or staged

As I said above, many people don't live in the houses they flip, so an empty home could indicate a flip. Or, if they do live there, you might see that the house has been "staged" to look warm and cozy for prospective buyers.

3. New surfaces

Are kitchen cupboards newly painted, or have they been re-faced, leaving the old cabinets behind? Is there drywall over existing walls, or new flooring on top of old? Can you spot layers on surfaces such as countertops or bathtub surrounds? There are many cover-up products on the market now, each one just as bad as the next.

4. "New" roof

Putting down another layer of bottom-grade asphalt shingles is a favorite trick. It looks nice, but how long will it last? You should never see more than two layers of shingles. If you do, you know that the roof needs to be stripped down and redone — which gives you some negotiating leverage.

5. Old mechanicals

People who flip houses are known for ignoring things like aging furnaces, electrical, and plumbing. Look closely at the age of the furnace. Especially when you see new bathrooms or a new kitchen, you want to have a licensed plumber and a licensed electrician come in to determine the quality of the work. On your first walk-through, look under sinks — is the plumbing still old while the sink and faucet have been replaced with new ones?

6. Shoddy finishes

This is probably the biggest sign. Look at the quality of the drywall: Can you see seams? Are the corners finished well? Examine the carpentry on window and door trims, baseboards, and cabinetry: Is everything square, level, flush, neatly joined? Do doors open and close properly?

I don't want you to get paranoid when you're going through houses, but I do want you to be cautious. Buying a flip — as great as it may look — can be a big mistake that you'll regret for years to come. Ask questions, look at the details — don't be fooled. And always ask to see permits for all renovation work.

Case Study #2
Eyes Wide Open

I always say that anything is possible in a renovation — anything. When I went to inspect this midtown Toronto house, I found a young couple who believed that, too.

When a young couple purchased this home less than two years ago, they didn't have many options. They were looking for something affordable in a neighborhood fairly close to where they worked in the downtown core. Toronto real estate prices have skyrocketed even higher since then, making it harder and harder for first-time buyers to enter the market.

They decided on this fixer-upper mostly because they could afford it. Because not that many "upgrades" had been done over the years, they could really see — with some help from a pretty decent home inspector — what they were getting. They didn't have to pay extra for previous renovations that might or might not have been done right — nobody had really messed with the house. Best of all for this ambitious couple, they could renovate to their hearts' content and fix it up just they way they wanted it.

I'm not usually in favor of homeowners taking on major renovation projects, because it's usually more than they can handle. But when I saw that this couple was making smart decisions — getting permits for everything, hiring licensed specialists for the parts they couldn't do (like plumbing and electrical) — and getting amazing results (just wait till you see their bathroom), I was impressed.

They bought this house with their eyes wide open, and now they're doing their best, even on a budget, to make everything right. What I like is that they're fixing it up for themselves, properly, so when they go to sell it at some point in the future, they will really be passing on good value. It's exactly the opposite of a flip.

An inspection on a house like this should turn up a lot of problems. On an older house, one that hasn't been very well maintained, that's to be expected. Some things you're likely to see: no insulation, windows needing to be replaced, electrical and plumbing in need of upgrading, the roof probably ready to be replaced. If you're looking for a fixer-upper, these are not the kinds of things that should turn you off. As long as you're realistic about what has to be done — and how much it's going to cost — the problems in a house like this are not really problems. As these homeowners told me, there weren't any big surprises when they had this home inspected, nothing to keep them from making an offer.

The inspection on this house showed some pretty obvious things. The electrical was all knob and tube, which the new owners couldn't get insurance for, so they had to have the whole house rewired. They got a permit and hired a licensed electrician, who did a really good job.

They were also told that the boiler was still functioning but was really old and not likely to last much longer. The pump broke down during their first winter, so they had it repaired and are hanging on to the old boiler for a little longer. A flat section of roof had to be redone, which the buyers discovered after they bought the house. The inspector said he couldn't access the roof because it was too high, so he wasn't able to give them an opinion about that flat part.

There were some details missed by this home inspector, but in general he gave these people good advice. His report stated that the house would require at least $50,000 worth of repairs in the first five years, which is probably accurate. Just to maintain the property at the level it was at, his report stated, would cost this couple between $1,500 and $2,500 per year. But why would they want to do that? The condition it's in right now wouldn't satisfy most people. (The previous homeowner, who'd been there for more than 25 years, is obviously an exception.)

FOUNDATION ISSUES

What the inspection report said: "Requires parging/repair at side"

Walking around the outside of the house, we see some deterioration on the foundation wall. It's probably all cinder block, which I like, but it was parged years ago to cover up the cracks and to make it more watertight. Over time parging breaks down, as you can see here, and then somebody goes in and tries to repair just a little bit at a time. The paint needs to be scraped down and any loose bits have to be removed, then the whole thing should be re-parged with a good bonding agent in the parging.

NO FLASHING BETWEEN SIDING AND ROOF

What the inspection report said: "Repair/replace all flashings with next roof covering replacement" There's no flashing underneath the siding to the roof line, just some caulking along the side. That can lead to a huge critter problem (not to mention water damage), so I'd get someone to address that ASAP. If any animals get in there, they'll make a mess in the wall and chew up the electrical.

WINDOWS IN NEED OF ATTENTION

What the inspection report said: "Window refurbishing/replacement recommended; upgrade caulking/painting"

Some original wood-frame windows remain, with aluminum storm windows, but even the ones that have been replaced are not that new anymore. The majority of the newer windows have fixed (inoperable) uppers with side sliders below — the cheapest windows you can buy. The exterior casings are showing signs of big problems, which will need to be addressed when the insulbrick is removed and replaced with siding of some kind. The leaded glass windows (on the left) are a nice touch in the living room, but they need some maintenance. The frames should be sanded down, painted, and caulked.

WINDOWSILL DETERIORATION

What the inspection report said: "Mortar repair recommended at various locations"

I really don't like to see a window-sill like this. It's brick, which is a very porous material; even worse is the mortar between the bricks — you can see that it's falling apart. Precast concrete sills, in one solid piece, are much better because there are fewer opportunities for water to get in and for sub-zero temperatures to cause cracks and crumbling. If the owners can't afford to entirely replace the sills right now, there are products on the market that can be used over top of them, which I would recommend. At least the top should be done to stop any more water penetration.

ADDITION DONE IN LOWER-QUALITY MATERIALS

What the inspection report said: "New wall covering/re-cladding recommended at rear"

We see a lot of this insulbrick asphalt siding on older homes. It was intended as a type of insulation (though the R-value is pretty low), and it supposedly made the house look like brick. For some reason a lot of people build additions with lower-quality materials and with less care than in the original house. I think sometimes people tried to do these things themselves, but they just don't stand the test of time the way the main brick house will.

Here we can see the siding beginning to deteriorate pretty badly, and whoever did it did not flash the bottom or between the wall and the covered entry roof, which can create huge water problems. We also see that the window was provided with a creative drip edge — this is not how it should be done.

SHARED GARAGE, WITH ROOF DETERIORATION AND ROTTED WALLS

What the inspection report said: No comment

This old garage is beyond repair. It's going to need to come down. I've seen these old structures a million times: they're built directly on the ground, where the moisture just rots everything out. Given the condition of the roof and the exterior walls, the only thing holding this structure up is the center wall.

To replace this garage will be interesting, because the owners will have to work with their neighbors, who own the other half of the building. They'll have to look into the city regulations to find out if they can put up a carport, which they want to do because it would be much less expensive. A garage would be worth more to them for resale, of course, but they have to determine how much they can afford to spend on one.

IMPROPERLY TILED STAIRS IN MUDROOM

What the inspection report said: No comment

This is a good example of why I don't like DIY. Someone put about ¾ inch of mortar directly over wooden stair treads. And it's not even floor tile—it's wall tile, which isn't thick enough to take the abuse of people walking on it. It's also far too slippery.

BASEMENT BATHROOM: AN ELECTRICAL AND PLUMBING DISASTER

What the inspection report said: "Both bathrooms poor; major work recommended"

Everything about this little basement bathroom is wrong. It was probably sold as a feature of the house, since extra bathrooms are a nice thing to have. But everything was done incorrectly. Look at this outlet — not a GFCI outlet — right next to the toilet. There is another ungrounded outlet — right next to the sink. This is a very unsafe situation.

I also discovered serious issues with the plumbing. When I looked at the plumbing stack and the laundry plumbing on the other side of the bathroom wall, I could see that nothing was vented properly. That's no doubt why the owners sometimes smelled sewer gas. This bathroom is not a benefit — it's actually the opposite. It needs to be gutted completely.

EFFLORESCENCE ON FOUNDATION WALLS: MOISTURE ALERT!

What the inspection report said: "Foundation wall interiors not accessible for inspection; recommend expose foundation walls and correct problem as needed"

When the inspection was done on this house, all the walls were studded and drywalled for a so-called finished basement, but even from the inspector's short note you can see that he had his suspicions that behind those walls things weren't right. The dampness and mustiness, which were both noted in the report, were a giveaway. With the drywall now removed, we can see

by the amount of efflorescence (salt deposits) just how much moisture must be coming through these walls all the time.

Instead of finishing this basement space and putting up a vapor barrier of any kind, I'd recommend cleaning up the wall and then having it re-parged by someone who's really good. This wall is fine as old basement walls go, but it needs to be left open so it can breathe, not be trapped in plastic.

MINIMAL WATER INTAKE; NO SHUT-OFF; LOW WATER PRESSURE IN HOUSE

What the inspection report said: "Location of main shut-off valve not determined; poor water pressure"

This is the main water intake, where the municipal water comes into the house. It's really old, so of course it's only a ½-inch pipe. The owners confirmed that they find the water pressure pretty inadequate. The strange thing is that there doesn't appear to be a shut-off valve or lever on this intake pipe; there should be one before the meter, which in this case would mean it should be close to the ground. I don't like the fact that the owners have no control over their water supply; they should have it checked out by a licensed plumber. And, very likely, the whole supply line from the house to the street should be replaced with a larger copper line, since right now it's probably outdated galvanized piping that's all clogged up with minerals.

As the supply lines continue, they are wrapped in old newspaper, as some kind of attempt at insulation. Not great, but that's what was often done in the days before insulation technology had really developed. We can even see when it was done: it was 1938, and Eaton's was selling chocolatey cream wafers.

UNSAFE BANISTER

What the inspection report said: "Loose rails/spindles/minor repair"

Just looking at it, you can't see what a problem this railing is. But if you try to put your hand on it as you walk up those top steps, you'll see the problem. The railing is no longer anchored securely where it attaches to the wall, which is making it loose and unsteady. The owners will have to make sure this is fixed properly — and soon.

PLASTER CEILINGS: EXPOSED, COVERED UP — NEEDING ATTENTION

What the inspection report said: "Ceilings in fair condition; need minor repairs"

Old plaster-and-lath ceilings are going to show their age. The first image shows the ceiling in one of the second-floor bedrooms, with obvious repairs to the plaster. Over time plaster can dry out and begin to pull away from the lath. In the hallways, the previous owner covered up the crumbling plaster by putting up an acoustic tile ceiling. It doesn't suit the character of an older home — and I'm never in favor of cover-ups.

UPSTAIRS KITCHEN ABOVE MUDROOM: ANOTHER PLUMBING DISASTER

What the inspection report said: "Marginal condition: major remodeling is recommended in the near future"

The new owners are fairly certain that this house was rented out as a couple of units, with a single entrance for both. This second-floor kitchen, now in the process of being dismantled, was used for one rental unit. It's tiny and not well heated, it has very little cupboard or counter space, and there's another ungrounded receptacle right near a water source. The new owners don't intend to rent out an illegal apartment, so they'll remove this kitchen and turn it into a sunroom — a much better use for it.

EVEN THE BEDROOMS NEED WORK: WALLPAPER MANIA

What the inspection said: No comment

This is not the kind of thing that home inspectors typically comment on, and I don't blame them. They make note of the condition of walls, but they don't comment on the cosmetic features. Here's the reality: if you like old houses, you have to like getting rid of wallpaper too, or else have the money to pay someone to remove it.

Once you get those layers off (and believe me, "dry-strippable" wallpaper was not being used when this house was built, so it's going to be a time-consuming job), you might discover that the walls are so cracked and scarred that they need a skim coat of plaster to make the room look as good as new again. If you happen to be gutting the space — in a bathroom, for instance—your job is much easier, and you have the opportunity to fix any other problems.

The new owners were thinking of putting drywall over the plaster — the time being spent on wallpaper removal was getting to them — but I think that's a cover-up to avoid. Unless all the trim and baseboards are removed and then put back on properly afterwards, it will be very obvious that the new layer has been added.

MAKING IT RIGHT: A HIGH-QUALITY BATHROOM RENOVATION

The new owners really impressed me. When I saw this second-floor bathroom — their main bathroom — I knew they were doing things the right way. Bit by bit they're bringing some quality back to this home.

To do this makeover, they gutted the bathroom completely, right down to the framing. That means they even removed the old pine floorboards. They needed insulation, ⅝-inch plywood, and cement board as a base for

the heated floor they wanted. They hired a licensed plumber to do all-new plumbing into this room, and of course the whole house was rewired by a licensed electrician. The wife did all the tile work on the walls and floors herself — and did a fantastic job, way better than most of the DIY I see out there. She really did her homework before trying this.

This bathroom is just fabulous. I really applaud these homeowners for what they've done. My recommendation: keep up the good work, and take lots of before, during, and after photos so that when they're ready to sell this house, they'll have a visual record of what they've done. That kind of documentation should be part of every selling package.

I don't make any bones about what I think of most do-it-yourself projects. Most people overestimate — by a long shot — how much they can do themselves.

The fact is that almost every home renovation job requires the kind of skill that comes only with training (either formal schooling or on-the-job training with the pros) and experience. These jobs also require high-quality and expensive tools — and a whole lot of time. I've fixed so many botched jobs done by well-meaning but incompetent weekend warriors that I don't recommend DIY as a smart or economical course of action.

But there are ways to get involved in a renovation, even doing some of the things yourself, if you follow certain guidelines. I'm warning you, though: this might not look like a big list, but it is!

1. Take it slow.
I hear a lot of people say they want something done fast and cheap. Unfortunately, that combination will always give you crappy results. Accept the fact that a renovation will take a lot of your time, no matter how much or how little you get involved. Just finding the right contractor (or subcontractors, if you're acting as your own general contractor) should take you at least as long as the work itself.

2. Know your limits.
Structural carpentry, electrical, plumbing, HVAC — these are areas for the pros only. Your job is to hire right and make sure you're getting the professional-quality work that you're paying for.

3. Play it safe, and work together with your contractor.
Maybe you've agreed with the contractor that you'll do all the demolition work before he gets there to start the job. Make sure that you know exactly what's needed, and that you have the proper equipment and safety gear.

Buying a house that needs a lot of work may be your only way into the housing market. Just make sure you know what you're getting into. Be realistic about what you're buying, how much it will really cost to bring it up to your standards, and how long it will take.

Case Study #3
New House,
Same Old Story:
Minimum Code Sucks

Think you can avoid problems by buying new? Think again.

There's good reason to be cautious: for one thing, minimum building code is nowhere near good enough. Second, these new housing developments go up so fast that quality and workmanship almost always suffer along the way — and sometimes the builders don't even meet minimum code. The lowest possible standard, and they don't meet it!

The first problem — inadequate minimum code — you can't do anything about. The second problem — shoddy workmanship — is exactly why you need a thorough home inspection on a brand-new house. And though many home inspectors will not guarantee that they can tell you if a building is up to code, on new-home inspections it is absolutely vital for them to do just that. You need to know if the house meets that bare-minimum standard.

Let's take a look at one house, built in 2006 by a builder with a good reputation. It's a decent house, and it looks nice. It has a brick veneer exterior, attractive pillars on the front porch, three bedrooms, three bathrooms (including an upgraded en suite bathroom), a second-story laundry room, and upgraded kitchen cabinets. But just like every other new home I see that's been built (almost) to minimum code, there are issues galore.

The builder had taken care of at least one obvious problem. The owners had paid for upgraded cabinet fronts, but the ones they got were so damaged that the home inspector stated in his report, "Very poor quality of finish on cabinets. Cannot believe these are upgraded cabinets." Good for him! Those comments helped the new homeowners get some satisfaction from their builder. In other words, the inspection gave the buyers some negotiating power, which is the main purpose of a new-home inspection — it's a form of protection.

But there were other problems that the inspector didn't notice. The new owners noticed, and they complained about them to their builder — who didn't want to fix them. "Bouncy floors" in the living room, which the inspector had noted before the owners moved in, were still a problem almost a year later when I was asked to take a look. Judging from the "repair" the builder had done, it was obvious the complaint wasn't being taken too seriously. It should have been, and I explained exactly why to the owners.

I looked through the whole house with them and identified other issues that they needed to take back to their builder. Minimum code is not a very ambitious target to aim for — you'd think the builders could do that much.

NO PLASTIC MEMBRANE ON FOUNDATION EXTERIOR

What the inspection report said: No comment

I do not see any dimpled plastic product (secondary membrane) on this foundation. They probably did only a sprayed foundation coating on this house. For a while the building code required builders to use a spray-on or roll-on coating on the exterior foundation walls, followed by a dimpled black plastic membrane. That second membrane was important for allowing the foundation some breathing room, and also for protecting the foundation coating when the stones and gravel were filled back in. But builders raised a big whoop about the added cost, saying that seamless concrete foundations made it unnecessary to have more than a single coating — and of course they'd use the less expensive one, the one that's really toxic. So the secondary membrane was taken out of code.

Since that happened, leaks in brand-new homes have been increasing like crazy, because that single layer isn't working. The owners will want to keep an eye on their foundation, especially from the inside, for the next couple of years. Minimum code is not going to keep their basement dry.

PRECAST EXTERIOR WINDOW SILLS: JOINED AND SEALED WITH MORTAR RATHER THAN CAULKING

What the inspection report said: No comment

It's nice to see they did concrete sills on the outside of the windows. I'd rather see continuous sills without joints, but if they're going to do it this way, they shouldn't fill the joints with mortar. When it rains, water will penetrate that mortar in minutes, get inside the wall, and eventually cause mold behind the wall. What they should have done is caulk it. The top section of the joint should be filled with a high-quality rubberized caulking to protect against rain and melting snow. Unfortunately, there are very few building inspectors who enforce this.

The builders will say, of course, that behind the brick, the wall is pro-

tected with a "rain-shed paper" (such as Tyvek or Typar), and that there's no need to worry if rain goes through that mortar. These are quality materials, but who says they're installed to be 100% watertight? Half of these guys don't even wrap their sills. If it's not completely sealed, water will penetrate and it will saturate this wall.

DRAIN CLEANOUT PROTRUDING FROM BASEMENT FLOOR

What the inspection report said: No comment

Building code requires that waste plumbing lines have a cleanout point every 20 feet. But why would the builder put this one right in the middle of the basement floor? If it absolutely has to be there, it should at least be cut down to floor level. Right now it is a serious tripping hazard. And with two little girls in the house, would you want to take a chance on having them trip and fall right onto a concrete floor?

"REPAIR" TO HOLE IN SUBFLOOR

What the inspection report said: No comment

An actual hole in the subfloor, and this is what was done to fix it! The owners saw this before the floor was finished — and they're pretty sure the builder would have just covered it up with carpet if they hadn't said anything. So this block of wood was nailed over the hole from the underside to plug it. It doesn't tie into anything structural on either side—it's relying on the OSB subfloor (the cheapest kind) to hold that wood in place. It's completely unacceptable.

MAIN FLOORS TOO "BOUNCY": NOT ENOUGH JOIST SUPPORT

What the inspection report said: "Floors bouncy in living room"

Even before they moved in, the owners knew they were going to have a problem with bouncy floors. It was even worse than they expected. If their daughter (only two years old at the time) ran through the living room, objects rattled on tables and glasses fell out of the china cabinet. They hoped that their builder would fix the problem, but after making a minor effort the company just brushed off its clients.

What I saw was definitely a problem. Today's minimum code requires that floor joists be at least 2 inches by 6 inches, depending on their span, and set 16 inches on center. They also need blocking or bridging (those cross-members of wood) every 4 feet — and that wasn't done here. Without that extra support, the floor has too much give to it, and that's why the owners are feeling the bounce. (In time, if enough people complain about problems, maybe the building code will actually change so that builders will need to set joists only 12 inches apart — that would be a big improvement.)

When the owners complained, the builder sent someone in to put in some bridging — those are the splintered-looking cross-members you can see in the photo. But they don't reach from top to bottom of the joist, so they're not really doing much. Some lengths of wood were also added from end to end, but again it's just a Band-Aid fix. These joists should have been blocked right in the first place, or doubled up (sistered) to make them stronger.

The builders did make a good suggestion: the owners could get ¾-inch hardwood installed in their living room, which would stiffen the floor. But guess who pays for that extra? You got it — the owners.

CROWNS DOWN: SAGGING FLOOR IN ENTRANCE HALL
What the inspection report said: No comment

Something that every pro knows is that you must have all crowns up when you're building a floor. "Crown" refers to the natural curvature in the wood. It's not like a warp or a twist, but there is a visible bow, and it's important. The crown indicates the way the wood will continue to move over time. So if you're trying to support a floor, do you want the floor to have a downward movement or do you want that wood to fight the pull of gravity? Of course you want the fibers of the wood itself to be resisting that downward pull. So crowns must always go up. (In walls, all the crowns should face out.)

In this house, the owners noticed that the floor in their foyer, which had a step up to the main level, dropped by about ¼ inch after they took possession. They complained, and the builder says he's coming back in to fix it. But unless he rips the whole area out and starts over again, he's not going to fix it.

It would have been so easy to avoid a problem like this: the crowns should have been marked, and they should have faced up. And in this one area under the step, the joists should have been tripled up rather than just doubled. How much would one more 12-foot length of 2×8 have cost?

FOUNDATION REPAIR: FUTURE MOISTURE PROBLEMS?

What the inspection report said: "Exposed basement concrete damaged by machinery; pitted; requires parging from bottom of brickwork to finished concrete"

Most of the poured concrete foundation inside the basement looked really good, but this one section was damaged at the time of the initial inspection. The builder repaired it because of the inspector's observations and the homeowners' complaints.

The new section didn't crumble when I tapped it with a hammer and dug into it with a pry bar, so it looks like it's adhering properly to the rest of the concrete around it. The problem with doing a repair like this is that it's a prime area for moisture to get in, unless it was sealed properly from the outside. It probably wasn't, because the exterior foundation was already done and we're fairly sure that the waterproofing out there is inadequate.

And, of course, I don't like the way the builders left these nails just sticking out of the wall. Obviously it's just not safe. This was another careless repair.

ELECTRICAL BOX IN COLD AIR RETURN

What the inspection report said: No comment

This is about as basic as it gets: you are not supposed to have a light fixture in a cold air return. What you're seeing here is an electrical box for the bathroom that's visible from the master bedroom. It should be obvious to anyone that pulling moist air through the system right across electrical is a bad idea.

Do I have to add that this does not meet building code?

SECOND-FLOOR LAUNDRY: NOT EVEN TO CODE
What the inspection report said: No comment

I would never recommend putting a washer and dryer on the second floor, but that's the trend right now. Because there's so much water going through a room like this, you need to make it a watertight zone. You need some type of membrane on the floor that reaches up behind the drywall. By lifting up the vent cover and looking at what's under the floor, I could tell there was no membrane.

But that led me to another problem: that vent cover should never have been on the floor. What good is a watertight zone if water can just flow over the floor and down the vent to the furnace? Another good question: why isn't the plumbing going through the wall rather than under the floor? Again, building code is the absolute minimum that builders should be delivering in a new home.

If this room leaks, there will be so many problems — which might be covered by the owners' insurance, but then their premiums will go up. The owners shouldn't have to worry about this!

INADEQUATE BATHROOM FAN
What the inspection report said: No comment

Bathroom fans are important for removing the moisture that we put into a house. Minimum code states that you need either an exhaust fan, one that pulls 50 cfm for a switched fan or 20 cfm for a fan that's always on, or a window, or both, depending on where you live. Because there's a window here, they can put in this ridiculous fan, the cheapest on the market, and the owners can't complain. A fan like this just pushes the air around and does not actually pull it out.

If you hold a tissue over the cover of a fan that's running and the tissue doesn't stay in place, you know the fan isn't strong enough to do any good at all.

SLOPPY FINISHES ON DOORS AND TRIM

What the inspection report said: "Typical flaws"

I refuse to call these kinds of things "typical." There's no need for unfinished edges, sloppy drywall mud work, and corners that aren't even square. When finishing is done like this, you can tell that it's just a cover-up for all the garbage that's behind the wall — and not even a very good cover-up.

 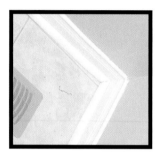 

COLD AND GAS ISSUES IN THE GARAGE

What the inspection report said: No comment

The garage is a cold zone: an area that doesn't have heat pumped into it during the winter, or air conditioning during the summer. But more often than not these days, the garage is integrated right into the structure of the house, which means there are some special requirements for doing it right. The biggest worry is that fumes from a running vehicle could enter the house. The second biggest concern has to do with cold — or, more accurately, how cold the room above the garage is.

The whole system for garages as recommended by the building code is doomed to fail. I've seen it again and again: R-20 insulation and taped drywall are not enough to keep those gases from seeping into the house. What's usually above the garage? A hot air vent and a cold air return. What happens when we turn on our car in the garage? Even with the garage door open, exhaust fumes can go right up into the cold air return and then into our furnace, which distributes that contaminated air all through the house.

The only way to do this right — and this should be building code — is to use a thermal break. That means at least 4 inches of high-density polyurethane insulation in the ceiling and 3 inches in the walls. This should be sprayed on everywhere. Because it creates an intimate contact wherever it's sprayed, there's no chance for air or gases to get in there.

In this garage I found a number of problems, things that showed that the builder didn't even meet the standards of the building code. First, to keep gases from entering the house, every drywall seam should be taped and mudded with at least two coats of plaster. Here it's pretty obvious that we have only one coat.

Second, take a look at the void in one corner of the garage. That leads up into a little girl's bedroom. Is that void blocked off by something more than a subfloor? How much cold is being let in there? How much contaminated air? This is a serious issue. Also, the outlet box has been caulked around the plate but it's still not properly sealed.

Now check out the garage door. It's the cheapest door on the market, the kind many builders use — in fact, you can't even buy it in stores. This is not a thermal door — in other words, it will not stop any cold from coming in. It's made with nothing more than medium-density fiberboard (MDF) with Plexiglas for the windows.

People need to be educated better about houses, and builders need to build better. On the other hand, if the minimum code lets builders get away with this, why should they do it any differently?

SHOULD YOU BUY NEW?

If you've recently bought a brand-new house or you're thinking of buying one, I know exactly what's going through your head: you don't want to buy any problems. Why should you buy yesterday's problems, somebody's reno gone wrong, or a house that's been flipped? And you're absolutely right: why should you buy a headache?

But the problem with the "let's buy new" way of thinking, as I've just shown you, is that many of today's new homes are not going to be problem-free.

It's easy to pinpoint the source of the problems. Builders are using the minimum building code as their guideline — and many parts of the building code are completely inadequate if you want a home that will last. Not only that, sometimes the builders (or their subcontractors) are not even meeting the bare-minimum standard.

WHAT'S THE PROBLEM WITH MINIMUM CODE?

First of all, let's go over what the building code is. It's a series of regulations set out by states across North America. Making sure new buildings and renovations meet the building code is the reason that permits and building inspections are required. The building code may vary somewhat from one place to the next, especially if an area has special concerns (flooding, termites, earthquakes, extreme cold, etc.), but in general it's pretty uniform. I've worked across Canada and in the U.S. as well, so I know that there are more similarities than differences when it comes to building code.

What's good about the building code is that, if it's followed, your house will not fall down. The electrical will not cause the house to go up in smoke. The plumbing will be good enough to keep your house from being flooded by broken pipes. But will the home stay dry and mold-free? Will the materials used to build it still be good in 50 or a 100 years? Will it be as energy-efficient as possible? No, no, and no.

The building code establishes the absolute minimum standard for how houses and other buildings should be constructed. That does not mean this standard is the best, or that it's recommended. It's not. In fact, building to this standard is what you can get away with legally, but other than that it's a joke: it's not the way to build something that lasts. I always recommend exceeding the requirements of minimum code and using better, more environmentally friendly materials.

BUILDERS ARE NOT REALLY THE BAD GUYS

Most builders I know are doing their best to construct homes that give you good value for your money. They have their reputations to think about too, and they want to be known as builders of quality homes, not as con artists. But they're in business to make a profit, just like anyone else, and building to minimum code helps them do that: the materials and methods just aren't as expensive that way. It's legal, so they do it.

Builders also have a lot of people working for them, so many that it's hard to really achieve quality control. There are always a lot of subcontractors on big builds in new housing developments, and lots of workers who don't last long on the job — so can the builders really guarantee the skill and integrity of every person who works on every house? No, they can't.

Those contractors and subcontractors are also working on deadlines and trying to maximize their profit for every day of work. When people rush, they get sloppy. They shouldn't, but they do. I see it all the time.

Materials delivered to a new building site may be left outside—exposed to the elements—for weeks or even months before being used. Some houses end up being built with warped, damaged wood. Others will have excess moisture issues that may never be resolved.

SHOULDN'T BUILDING INSPECTORS CATCH MOST PROBLEMS IN NEW HOUSES?

Earlier in this book I explained the difference between building inspectors and home inspectors. Building inspectors work for the government and are there to inspect new homes and renos to make sure they conform to building code (some issues, such as bouncy floors, are the result of problems in the building code, and the inspector cannot rectify them). Home inspectors work privately and are there to help buyers and sellers understand what's good and what's bad about a home.

In theory, every new home will be looked at thoroughly by a building inspector. If the inspector finds that building code hasn't been met, he or she can give the house a failing grade and repairs will have to be made.

In practice, it's possible that not every house gets a real inspection. There are never enough inspectors to check out all the new houses being built. In a new development, inspectors will often look at just a "representative sample" of houses and then assume that all the other houses are about the same.

WILL A NEW HOME WARRANTY PROTECT YOU? DON'T COUNT ON IT.

Unfortunately, not all states have warranty programs that protect home-owners from shoddy building practices. (Mistakes can happen, and even in a well-built home it may take awhile for a problems to arise. For example, a problem with a heating system might not be evident until the weather turns cold.) Upstanding new-home builders will give you a warranty whether or not it is mandated by your state. Ask you real estate agent about the law in your location.

Wherever you live, a warranty program is supposed to protect people who buy new homes. The program should provide deposit protection and protection against defects in work and materials, unauthorized substitutions, and delayed closing or delayed occupancy without proper notice. Some people say that these programs work. In my experience, though, too many buyers are left high and dry, with expensive problems to fix and no one to push the home builder.

Another problem is the time limit on programs. Coverage length varies, and sometimes it's not long enough for most real problems to show themselves. By the time you discover a "defect in work or materials," the limit has likely passed, and the builder is off the hook.

IS THERE A SOLUTION TO PROBLEMS WITH NEW HOMES?

The best solution would be higher standards for the building code and more building inspectors to ensure rigorous inspections. But until that happens, there are things you can do.

If you are going to buy a newly built home, be cautious. Do your homework on the builders — go to other developments they've built and talk to people who've bought their homes. That's right: knock on doors. Ask if the house was done on time. Were there problems? Are there any issues the owners are worried about? If the owners had any complaints about their house, did the builder deal with them quickly, properly, and without a hassle?

Then, if you find a builder that seems to work with integrity and does quality work, find the best home inspector you possibly can before you finalize the purchase and move in. Make sure you check out the inspector by contacting a lot of people he or she has worked for. Find someone with experience, someone whose judgment you can trust.

Then, when you move into that new home, take photographs of everything. Document everything. If you can see problems, tell your builder about them.

Do not rest until you get satisfaction. At the least — the very least — your builder should be providing you with a home that meets the minimum building code in every single way. But even that's not saying much.

Case Study #4
Making It Right
on a Century Home

When you're thinking of buying an older home, what are the most important things to look for? What if you want to maintain an older home properly?

When it comes to an old home, especially one as old as a hundred years or more, you know for a fact that the house has had some work done on it, probably a lot over the years. So my main concern is this: how skilled were the people who did the work? That's something you can judge by how well the work is holding up. If it's been done recently, within the last twenty years or so, you'll want to see permits.

I went through the following house to help the owners find problems in their home and to give them some advice on how to prioritize their maintenance plans for the future. Home inspections can be really useful for this — if you find a knowledgeable inspector.

This is an older home, built in 1903, in a mature and very desirable part of Toronto. From the outside, you can see that it's a fine old place with lots

of character. But along with character, old houses also have unique maintenance issues.

WOOD MAINTENANCE

There's a lot of wood on the exterior, with cedar shingles on one side of the house and on the roof of the side entrance, wood framing around the windows, and some Tudor-style half-timbering over stucco. Maintaining that wood is definitely going to be a concern for the future. You can see moss growing on some areas of the cedar shingles, which is a sign of a fair bit of moisture — those shingles will need to be replaced before any others. The half-timbered sections on the cupola will also need to be watched: the flat, horizontal surfaces of the wood members are prime locations for rot and for moisture to penetrate the wall.

PORCH MAINTENANCE

The porch pillars are made from a different brick from the rest of the house, which might mean that the originals were replaced at some point. Whatever the case, they're in good shape, and I like to see those weep holes near the bottom of the wall: these are for water to escape after rain or snow has penetrated the brick. I noticed some issues with the mortar between the bricks. When mortar crumbles and falls apart, it has to be repointed by someone who knows how to do it right — it has to be scraped out to a depth of at least 3/4" and then filled back in.

As for the rail, spindles, and wood decking, they're in really good shape right now. They have to be watched for cracking or peeling paint, because that's an opportunity for water to get in and cause rot. Any painted wood on an exterior should be touched up or completely repainted every few years — but it has to be scraped, sanded, and primed before any new paint goes on.

BRICK FOUNDATION

Another issue is going to be the house's brick foundation. We can see that the whole structure is double-brick construction, because shorter bricks are showing up at regular intervals — there are two interlocking layers of brick, with a void on the inside as a breathable space. That means we have a very strong structure that's carrying the load of the house (unlike today's brick houses, which are really frame houses with a brick veneer or facade).

But the age of the building also means that the brick continues all the way into the ground — that's the way it was commonly done when this house was built. Brick is actually a very porous material that deteriorates when it's in contact with the ground all the time. That's why the building code was changed about 50 or 60 years ago so that all brick houses had to be set on a poured concrete or concrete block foundation and at least 8 inches off the ground.

The best approach to an old house like this is to get natural drainage working for you: keep the ground sloped away from the house so that water will run away from the brick after a rainfall. And watch for signs that the perforated pipe (probably clay on such an old home) is broken or blocked — if it is, you'll have serious water backing up through the basement walls, and this will have to be addressed by excavating and replacing the perforated pipe around the foundation.

HISTORICAL DETAILS PRESERVED AND OTHER DETAILS ADDED

At one time this house was used as a duplex, but previous owners turned it back into a single-family home. Those owners had a lot of work done, and they made sure that in at least some cases, the character of the house was maintained or returned to the original. I can see that the plasterwork on the ceiling has been redone in some places, but it was done right, by someone who knew what he was doing.

The high baseboards and wide casings around doors and windows are standard in older homes. These are original, though they were probably all unpainted oak at one time. They could be returned to their original look, but that's not necessary; it's just a matter of personal preference.

They eyebrow window in the master bedroom is just great. It's only a single layer of glass, so it's not the best for keeping the cold out, but its uniqueness makes it worth it. The owners should watch the interior wood for signs of water penetration or damage, and make sure that the exterior putty around the panes of glass is maintained.

The stained glass window in the stairwell suits the age of the house, and it blocks the view of the neighboring house, which is only a few feet away.

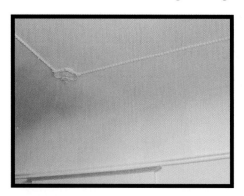

HEATING WITH HOT WATER

This house is still heated with hot water radiant heat. Many of the old radiators are still being used, but a new furnace was installed in the past couple of years, and some new radiators (thinner and taking up less space) were installed at the same time.

Some issues come up when you're replacing an old boiler. Normally, the old boilers had asbestos wrapped around the pipes. Asbestos doesn't hurt anybody as long as it's not touched. But when it is, it has to be done right, because asbestos fibers are released into the air and will lodge in the lungs, where they can be very harmful and even cause cancer. This should be done only by reputable contractors who are licensed to do asbestos removal. Then the new boiler can be installed.

The new boiler in this house is good. I can see that it was installed by a licensed gas fitter because it has all the proper labels on the gas lines; if it didn't have them, it would definitely raise an alarm for me. There are two things I don't like about what was done here. One, the furnace is vented together with the water heater. That's acceptable by code, but I don't like it — I'd rather see them vented separately.

Second, the old boiler must have been installed directly on the earth floor, and the cement floor was built up around it. When the old boiler was taken out, the installer should have filled in the gap on the floor so that the new furnace could sit on concrete rather than bare earth. Even using a couple of 2x2 patio stones would have been much better for the new furnace. Moisture comes up through the ground, and it will attack the metal. Because the installer couldn't be bothered to do it right, the life of this wonderful new boiler has been diminished a little.

The other maintenance issue with radiators is that they have to be "bled" periodically to release trapped air. If this isn't done, the hot water will be blocked and it won't warm up the radiators. Always check for leaks and rotting wood, and make sure the wood is properly protected with a waterproof finish.

ELECTRICAL: HOW MUCH HAS BEEN DONE?

There's no doubt an old house like this would have been wired originally with knob and tube. Even when people claim that the knob and tube has all been removed, I don't think I've found a house yet that doesn't still have some around. As I've said before, there is nothing really wrong with the knob-and-tube wiring, but it breaks down when we overload the circuits — and that's what happens with the kind of appliances we use today and how many of them we have.

We see a combination of things in this house: older, two-prong receptacles mounted on baseboards (maybe still knob and tube, but maybe not), along with some new electrical in parts of the house that have been renovated, and an electrical panel that's well labeled and neatly done. The panel is at least 10 or 12 years old, but everything I see shows that a licensed electrician has been here and cared about what he was doing.

If the owners wants to make sure their electrical is acceptable and safe throughout the whole house, they should do a couple of things. One, they should find out if permits were taken out for the electrical work that was done before they moved in. That's easy: you can just call the city and find out what they have on file. Two, they should bring in a licensed electrician to spend a day or two sourcing everything. He can give them an estimate of how much it would cost to replace the older parts of the wiring.

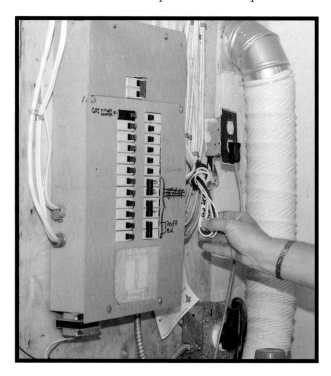

ALMOST UNFINISHED BASEMENT

Two rooms in this basement are "finished." This double-brick wall has been simply painted over. This is not bad — and I'd rather see this than a basement that has been finished incorrectly.

WINDOWS: INSTALLATION, INSULATION, AND MOISTURE ISSUES

There are a lot of newer windows in this house, installed before the current owners bought it. We don't know if proper foam insulation was put around these windows or if the installer used some batt insulation — or maybe he used none at all.

We can see some plaster deterioration under windows. That's a sign that the older windows allowed water to get in and damage the plaster. Now that new windows are in, the source of the moisture is probably not a concern anymore, but the owners should make sure that the caulking on the outside of the windows is still in perfect shape. To fix the plaster, they need to do more than just put a trowel-load of filler over it — new plaster will not stick to old, deteriorated plaster. The owners need to remove all this old plaster, right down to the lath, and put in a new layer of hard, durable plaster such as Dur-abond-90. Otherwise, it will keep peeling every time they paint it.

Of course, if the owners update other windows throughout the house, they should make sure they are properly installed, with foam insulation and a high-quality rubberized exterior caulking.

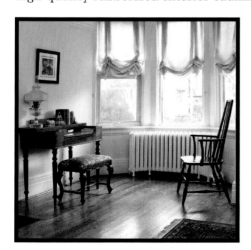

RENOVATED KITCHEN

The kitchen was redone by the current owners about three years ago. They had the cabinets and appliances replaced and a new limestone floor laid.

I could tell from the height of the transition strip from the kitchen floor to the dining room that the new floor was laid over a substantial subfloor, or maybe even over an existing floor. The owner confirmed that the existing floor had been left in place, and though I don't usually recommend covering up an old floor, in this case it's not a bad thing because it's providing a lot of stability for that new tile.

The part I like best about this kitchen renovation was that the owners got lots of references before hiring their contractor, and they got permits for all the work. Updated plumbing, updated electrical — everything was done by licensed professionals.

TIME FOR BATHROOM RENOVATIONS?

There are four bathrooms in this house. The powder room on the main floor is in fine shape, the one in the basement needs a complete overhaul, and the two four-piece bathrooms (one in the master suite and one for the kids) are close to needing renovations as well. There are issues with cracking grout, caulking not done right, and musty smells that probably indicate some moisture problems behind the walls. These bathrooms were probably done in the mid-'80s, so it's not surprising that they're in need of some help.

The owners could hold off on these, but the bathrooms will have to be redone. Moisture problems never fix themselves. And redoing the bathrooms will be an opportunity for the owners to do things in their own style.

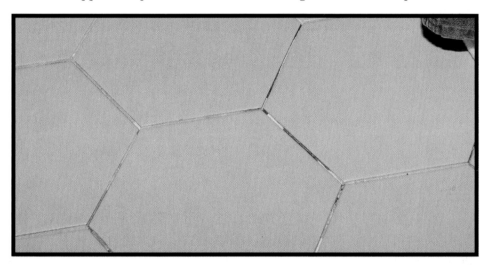

THE ATTIC MATTERS

Double-brick houses from a hundred years ago were not designed for insulation. They were designed to breathe from the outside to the inside and back again. Over time, people make the changes to these old houses, and usually they don't understand that you can't just apply today's minimum code and expect it to work properly. What we see in this house is that probably no one has tampered with the walls, and I'm glad to see that.

A problem that I do see, though, is with the attic. On a warm summer day, the thermographic imaging camera shows some very hot spots on the second-story ceiling. I couldn't get into the attic to check out the insulation situation because a previous owner had blocked off the attic access — which is a very bad idea. And when you look at the outside of the house, there are no visible vents to the attic — no roof vents, ridge vents, or gable vents. The soffits are fitted with perforated metal, but were holes drilled into the wood before those soffits were added? Is there any air circulating in that attic at all? The answer is no. So the attic is going to be holding all that heat from the outside and from the rest of the house.

What I'd like to see is a spray-foam polyurethane insulation on that attic floor, on the surface right above the second-story ceiling. That creates a thermal break — you're not allowing the heat from the house to go into the attic at all; you're keeping hot away from cold. That's going to prevent heat transfer and heat loss, and it's also going to prevent condensation.

The next part is also really important: you need some roof vents and gable vents to have enough airflow up there. Moving the air and moisture through the attic space is what keeps all the timbers and the roof healthy; it keeps them from deteriorating.

DINING ROOM: THE ONLY ORIGINAL ROOM IN THE HOUSE

The Tudor-style design of the house really shows in the dining room, where there's wood detailing on the ceiling and the walls. None of this is structural — it's all for aesthetics. The owners should maintain it exactly as they've been doing. The only changes they might consider will come up if they update all the electrical.

Overall, what I'm seeing in this house is that the right people have been in here. I have some concerns about electrical and about venting and insulation in the attic, but those are the only major issues. As with all older houses, maintenance is the key to keeping the value and protecting your investment.

SHOULD YOU BUY OLD?

I'm often asked if there has been a "golden age" of homebuilding. In other words, during what era were the best products and building practices used? What people are looking for is a recommendation about how old a house they should buy – new, a century home, 40 years old?

Honestly, there is no real golden age. Every house needs maintenance over time; every house will need upgrades and updates. Let's face it though: things wear out.

But if I were to identify the period of building I think was the best, I'd probably say the 10-year range between the mid-1950s and the mid-1960s. By today's standards, those homes are overbuilt, but I'd obviously disagree with that, since I think today's minimum building standards are not nearly high enough.

Older homes, like this beautiful one, have their complications, but many people want them for their looks. They are also usually found in the most desirable and established downtown areas. Yes, you can put a lot of money into maintaining an older home, but if you want character and beauty, it's probably worth it. And if you buy in a section of town where the demand remains steady over time, it's probably not a financial risk to invest a lot in that older house: you'll get it all back if and when you're ready to sell.

A FEW LAST WORDS

At the beginning of this book, I talked about what "normal" looks like these days when it comes to buying and selling homes. Every day, there are people buying houses and getting nasty surprises when they start living in them – even though they paid for the advice of a home inspector before the signed on the dotted line.

I don't like seeing and hearing those stories. They're frustrating because they just aren't necessary. High standards in the home inspection industry would go a long way toward helping people make informed decisions about the houses they buy. Because while it's normal for houses to need maintenance, upgrading, and sometimes even major repairs, it should never be normal to buy a house that has gotten a clean bill of health from a home inspector and then find out that you're going to be shelling out big bucks to make it dry, safe, and comfortable to live in.

By reading this book, you've taken the first step in reducing your chances of getting shocked like this. You've informed yourself about housing basics. You've learned why you need to look past the surfaces of a house to see what's behind them and behind the walls — the structure, plumbing, electrical, and HVAC. You can go into any home inspection with your eyes open, ready to see the challenges — and there will be challenges, with any house.

More than anything, I hope you've learned that home inspections are a vital, necessary part of buying or selling any house — but that you must demand the best. Before you commit yourself to buying and maintaining the most expensive purchase of your lifetime, shouldn't you talk to someone who can give you the benefit of experience and knowledge, and the good sense to bring in experts when they're needed?

Slow down, ask the right questions, and hire right — that's the key to protecting your hard-earned money, and your future.

CHECKLISTS

■ Questions to Ask Real Estate Agents

■ Questions to Ask Real Estate Agents' References

■ Documents to Provide When You're Selling Your Home

■ Questions to Ask Home Inspectors

■ Questions to Ask Home Inspectors' References

■ Questions Your Real Estate Agent Should Ask the Seller

■ Questions about the Exterior

■ Questions about the Basement and Mechanicals

■ Questions about the Interior

■ Questions about Condominiums

Use these checklists when you're finding a real estate agent or a home inspector, and use them as reminders when you're going through a home. No, these checklists don't take the place of an inspection report! They're here to help you remember some of the key points I've raised in this book, especially the red flags. Make sure you know the answers to these questions before you buy.

CHECKLIST #1
Questions to Ask Real Estate Agents

Whether you're selling or buying, hiring the right agent can be an important part of the home inspection process. Don't be afraid to ask lots of questions when looking for a real estate agent. Here are some of the key things to ask:

1. How long have you been working as a real estate agent?

_____
_____
_____

2. What's your area of expertise (condos, new homes, historic homes)?

_____
_____
_____

3. Do you specialize in listings in one geographic area or neighborhood?

_____
_____
_____

4. How many buyers/sellers have you successfully represented in the last six months?

_____
_____
_____

5. How will you protect my interests, and why should I hire you rather than another agent?

_____
_____
_____

6. Can you provide me with three to six references of people who have hired you in the past year? (Follow-up on these references is critical.)

_____
_____
_____

Questions to Ask Real Estate Agents' References

You should check three to six real estate agent's references — more if necessary. If you're buying a house, be sure that some of the references are from clients who have been in their house for at least one heating season.

1. Did your agent take the time to understand your needs and budget?

_____

_____

_____

2. Did you receive appropriate listings?

_____

_____

_____

3. How many houses did your agent show you?

_____

_____

_____

4. Did your agent ever tell you that you "could do better" or recommend you avoid a house after a showing?

_____

_____

_____

5. Did your agent ever pressure you to buy a house that you weren't certain of?

_____

_____

_____

6. Did you feel your agent was honest and trustworthy?

_____

_____

_____

CHECKLIST #3
Documents to Provide When You're Selling Your Home

The best "fluffing" you can do when you're selling your home is to give prospective buyers all the information they need to know. A good package will include:

❑ home inspection reports (a recent report and one from the time of your purchase)

❑ work permits and inspection reports for any work done during the time that you owned the house (and for any work done before, if you have documentation from the previous owners)

❑ "before," "during," and "after" photos for any renovations or repairs

❑ warranties for any new building materials (windows, siding, shingles, etc.)

❑ warranties and manuals for appliances included with the house (furnace, heat exchanger, water softener, water heater, air conditioner, kitchen appliances, etc.)

❑ copies of the previous year's utility bills, to give proof of heating and cooling costs

Questions to Ask Home Inspectors

Hiring the right home inspector could save you money, heartache, and nasty surprises. Don't be afraid to ask plenty of questions, including the following:

1. How long have you been working as a home inspector?

   _____
   _____
   _____

2. Did you have any experience in the building trades before becoming a home inspector? If so, what kind, and how much?

   _____
   _____
   _____

3. Do you belong to an association of home inspectors? Are you a certified member?

   _____
   _____
   _____

4. What kind of equipment do you use while inspecting (binoculars/ladder/ infrared thermographic imaging camera)?

   _____
   _____
   _____

5. Can you provide me with at least six references from people who have hired you in the past three years? (Following up on these references is critical, especially references from clients who have owned their homes for at least a year.)

   _____
   _____
   _____
   _____

CHECKLIST #5:
Questions to Ask
Home Inspectors' References

You should check three to six references — more if necessary. If you're buying a house, be sure that some of the references are from clients who have been in their homes for more than a year.

1. How did your home inspector check the roof, roofing systems, and chimney?

2. Did your home inspector show up on time? How long did the inspection last? Did the inspector encourage you to take part in it?

3. What tools did your home inspector bring? Did they include a thermographic imaging camera?

4. Did you feel that your home inspector explained the limitations of the inspection thoroughly?

5. Did your home inspector recommend other specialists to investigate any potential problems?

6. Have there been any surprises since you've moved in? Did your home inspector miss anything?

7. Did you feel your home inspector was honest and trustworthy?

Questions Your Real Estate Agent Should Ask the Seller

A home inspection can start even before your home inspector comes to look at the house. Here are some important questions your real estate agent should ask the seller to begin the process.

1. How long have you owned the house?

2. What was the purchase price?

3. What's the sales and renovation history of this house? What repairs or improvements have you made in the time you've owned it?

4. How old are the major structural and mechanical systems—roof, windows, furnace and air conditioning, plumbing, electrical?

5. Are there building permits and building inspection reports for all work done on this house (structural, plumbing, electrical)? (Ask to see any documents.)

6. Do you know if this house was a marijuana-grow operation at any time?

7. Have there been any problems with water and waste drainage?

8. Has the heating system been converted from oil? If so, what happened to the oil tank? (Was it buried on the property?)

9. Are there any rooms that require additional sources of heat?

10. If there is a functioning fireplace, has the chimney been cleaned on a yearly basis?

11. Were the fireplace and chimney properly installed by licensed technicians? When? (Ask to see installation certificates.)

12. What are the annual heating and cooling costs for this house? (Ask to see bills.)

CHECKLIST #7
Questions about the Exterior

This checklist doesn't replace a thorough home inspection by a good home inspector, but these are important questions to ask about a home you're considering buying.

YARD
- If there is fencing, what condition is it in?
- Are trees close enough to the house for roots to damage the foundation, or for branches to damage the roof or the gutters?

DRIVEWAY
- What material is the driveway, and what condition is it in?

ROOF
- What material is the roof, and what condition is it in?
- How old is the roof?
- Is there more than one layer of roofing material?
- Is there an uneven or sagging roof line?
- What type of flashing is around the base of the chimney? What condition is it in?
- What is the condition of the chimney (bricks/blocks and mortar) and chimney cap, if any?
- What is the height of the chimney in relation to the roof line?
- Are there enough roof vents and gable vents? Are any of them dented or blocked?
- Are all skylights double-glazed? Is there any condensation? Is the flashing properly fitted and well sealed?
- Is the dormer flashing adequate and properly installed?
- Are there enough downspouts connected to the gutters? Are they properly attached? Do they extend far enough from the foundation?
- What is the condition of the soffits, fascia, and gutters?

FOUNDATION AND STRUCTURE

- What type of foundation is there?
- Is there any buckling, bulging, leaning, or major cracks in the foundation walls?
- Are any wood members in contact with soil?
- Are all new or enlarged windows or doors framed and supported properly? Are there building permits and inspection reports for these additions?

SHEATHING (BRICK, SIDING, ETC.)

- What type of exterior sheathing is there?
- Are there any signs of moisture, rot, fungus, or other damage?

GARAGE

- What size is the garage (including the door) and what condition is it in?
- If the garage is attached, is there an adequate gas barrier between it and the house? Is there a fireproof door to the house? What condition is the door in?

PORCH/DECK/BALCONY

- What is the age and condition of the structure?
- Are any wood members in contact with soil?
- Is the structure properly attached to the main building?

CHECKLIST #8
Questions about the Basement and Mechanicals

Many of the important systems of a home are found in the basement. This checklist doesn't replace a thorough inspection by a good home inspector (and specialists, when necessary), but make sure you ask and understand the answers to these questions.

BASEMENT (UNFINISHED)

- Is there any evidence of moisture—mildew, mold, a musty smell, condensation on walls and windows, dampness in floors and walls, visible leaking from foundation cracks?

BASEMENT (FINISHED)

- Is there any evidence of moisture—mildew, mold, a musty smell, condensation on walls and windows, dampness in floors and walls, visible moisture of any kind?
- Are any wood or metal studs attached directly to exterior masonry walls? (If yes, check for signs of moisture on walls: mildew, mold, rust, dampness, a musty smell.)
- Is there any insulation on exterior walls? (2" rigid foam or polyurethane insulation is ideal as both thermal break and vapor barrier.)
- Is there insulation under finished flooring? (1" rigid foam board is best.)
- Are there adequate fire escape routes for any basement bedrooms?
- Are there enough heat ducts and a cold air return?
- Is the furnace big enough to heat the house?
- Is all new electrical or plumbing properly tied in to existing systems?
- Is the basement plumbing (toilet, sinks) vented properly?

BASEMENT STRUCTURE

- Do any walls appear to be buckling, bulging, or leaning? How extensively?
- Are there any major cracks (1/4" or more) running in more than one direction? (If yes, consult a structural engineer.)
- Are any joists sagging or not fully connected to the subfloor above?
- If joists have been given extra supports (e.g., jack posts), have these been installed properly and safely?
- Are there any notches or cracks in the joists?
- Is there any rotting wood in the joists or other supporting members?

ELECTRICAL

- Is the amperage high enough for needs of modern lifestyles?
- Is any knob-and-tube wiring still active?
- Has the electrical service or panel been changed in any way? (If yes, ask for permits.)
- Are there any hidden junction boxes?
- Are fuses or circuit breakers overloaded?
- Are there enough outlets throughout the house?
- Are all outlets near water sources properly grounded (GFCI)?

PLUMBING

- What material is used for supply lines?
- What material is used for waste lines?
- How big are the main supply lines?
- Is there adequate water pressure?
- Are there any signs of water or waste backing up?
- Do toilets and sinks drain quickly?
- Is the vent stack the correct height above the roof line?

WATER HEATER

- the water heater included with the house, or rented?
- Is it in good condition, and how old is it?
- Is it big enough?

HEATING, VENTILATION AND AIR CONDITIONING (HVAC)

- What type of furnace and heat distribution is there?
- How old is the furnace, and what is its life expectancy?
- When was the furnace last maintained?
- What is the condition of the oil tank (if any)?
- Are there any unused oil tanks in the basement or elsewhere on the property? (If yes, costly environmental cleanup could be needed.)
- What is the condition of the ductwork?
- Is there extra ductwork for an addition or a basement renovation?
- Are all vents open and receiving airflow?
- Are all rooms adequately heated?
- How old is the air-conditioning system, and what is its life expectancy?

CHECKLIST #9
Questions about the Interior

A thorough inspection of every room in the home can help you spot any potential issues. Some issues are more complex than others, and some may apply only to older homes, but don't hesitate to ask your home inspector the following questions:

FLOORS
- What is the type, age, and condition of finish flooring (room by room)?
- Are there multiple layers of flooring?
- What is the strength and condition of the subfloor?
- Do the floors bounce?
- Are the floors level?
- Do the floors slope towards the middle of the house, or towards the exterior walls?

WALLS
- Are there signs of water damage near windows, floor levels, corners, or ceilings?
- Are there signs that walls have been removed?
- Are there cracks in walls above windows or doors?
- What is the condition of the plaster or drywall?

WINDOWS
- Are there signs of water damage or wood rot on window frames and sills or on the walls below?
- What is the quality of the windows (number of panels of glass, type of hardware)?
- What is the condition and life expectancy of the windows?
- Do all windows have screens? Are they in good condition?

DOORS
- Do all doors swing and close properly?
- Do exterior doors have adequate protection (roof overhang of some kind) from the elements?
- Is there weatherstripping around exterior doors?

STAIRS

- Are there any visible gaps between the stair stringer and wall?
- Are the stairs too steep, or do they have narrow treads?
- Is the handrail shaky, too low, or absent?
- Are there any horizontal supports under the handrail, or any vertical spindles (balusters) more than 4 inches apart?

KITCHEN

- What is the type, quality and condition of cabinet carcases?
- What is the type, quality and condition of cabinet doors and finishes?
- Are the cabinets level, and their doors and drawers aligned?
- Are there any visible gaps between cabinets?
- Are there signs of moisture damage, such as rotted wood, especially under the sink?
- What is the type, quality and condition of counters?
- Are there any chips, cracks, stains, or gaps between seams?
- Is there enough counter space, especially next to the sink and range?
- Are there any signs of water damage to the underside of the kitchen counter near the sink?
- What is the age, quality, and condition of appliances (if included)?
- How good is the drainage from the kitchen sink?
- Are there any signs of leakage or previous water damage?
- Is there a window and/or exhaust fan in the kitchen?
- Does the fan vent outside (not to the garage or another room)?
- Is the fan powerful enough to remove moist air?
- Where does the central vac exhaust (hopefully not into the house)?

BATHROOMS

- Are there any signs of moisture damage—mildew, mold, a musty smell?
- Is there a window and/or exhaust fan in each bathroom?
- Do the fans vent outside?
- Are the fans powerful enough to remove moist air?
- Is there any softness or sponginess in the flooring (especially around the toilet) or the tiled walls?
- Is there a strong toilet flush?
- Is there good drainage from the bathtub and/or showers?
- Is there adequate storage?

ATTIC (UNFINISHED)

- Is there easy access to the space?
- What is the type, amount, and condition of insulation?
- Are there signs of moisture — condensation, mildew, rotted wood? (In cold weather, check for frost on roof sheathing above.)
- Is there adequate ventilation?

ATTIC (FINISHED)

- Does the attic conform to minimum building code specifications? (Ask vendors for building permits for attic conversion.)

Questions about Condominiums

Whether you're buying a new condominium or an older one, research the builder and the condominium development, and ask your real estate agent and home inspector plenty of questions, including these:

1. What restrictions apply to the exterior of the condominium (windows, window coverings, balconies, terraces)?

   _____

   _____

2. What is the monthly maintenance fee? How much reserve fund is allocated for the building?

   _____

   _____

3. What is the sales history of the development? Are the units primarily owner-occupied or investment properties?

   _____

   _____

4. For older developments, have there been any special levies to cover repairs that weren't covered by the monthly maintenance fee?

   _____

   _____

5. Have there been any major repairs to the condominium? Are there any under way now?

   _____

   _____

6. What other development is planned in the neighborhood? (In a condo tower in an urban area, this is an important question — you don't want your priceless view of the city be blocked by another condo tower.)

   _____

   _____

7. Can I see the minutes from the condo board meetings?

   _____

   _____

GLOSSARY

A

ABS (acrylonitrile butadiene styrene) Hard black plastic plumbing pipes, used primarily for drainage. The rule for drainage pipes is to use ABS pipes in your house and PVC for in-ground pipes. Some municipalities forbid the use of ABS pipes for any application.

B

beam
A wooden or steel member that runs perpendicular to the joists, helping to support the structure above.

board-and-batten
Exterior siding made of wide vertical boards with narrow strips of wood (battens) covering the joints between them.

brick veneer
A layer of real brick applied to the exterior walls of a house that is framed using some other material, usually wood. Solid brick houses are most often built of two layers of brick with an air space in between.

building inspector
A municipal employee who inspects a home as it's being built or renovated to ensure that the work meets the minimum local building code.

built-up roof
A flat roof covered with layers of tarpaper, tar, and gravel. These first-generation flat roofs have been largely replaced by seamless, rubberized membrane roofs.

C

casing
The framing members that go around a door or window. Usually made of wood, on exterior walls they should be protected by waterproof caps, with drip caps along the top edge.

clapboard
Traditional exterior wood siding made of horizontal boards with overlapping edges.

column
A vertical post made of wood, steel, or masonry (concrete block, brick, or poured concrete) that helps support the structure above. Columns are usually found in the basement but can also be used in place of structural walls on other levels of a house; in such cases, they are carrying the load of the walls and floors in a more or less straight line down to basement columns and the footings below.

D

dormer
An upright window (and its supporting structure) that projects from a sloping roof to provide light and headroom for the top floor of a house.

downspout
A vertical metal or plastic pipe that carries water from the gutters to the ground.

E

eaves
The undersides of a roof where they project past the edge of the house.

gutter
A horizontal trough attached to the eaves or fascia that collects water from the roof and carries it to the downspout.

efflorescence
An accumulation of white crystalline salts on masonry walls. This mineral residue is what's left after moisture has evaporated.

F

fascia
Long, flat boards fastened to the ends of the roof rafters at the eaves, on the exterior of the house. It is usually protected by aluminum capping, though traditional fascia may be painted wood.

fiber cement siding
An exterior wall covering made of a mixture of cement, sand, and cellulose fibers.

flashing
Thin, L-shaped sheet metal used to prevent water leakage around chimney, dormers, skylights, and other structures protruding from the roof. The upright part should rest flush against the structure, with exterior caulking to fill any gaps, while the flat part should run under the surrounding shingles.

flue
The metal pipe inside a chimney that carries gases from the furnace (or smoke from a fireplace) outside the house.

footings
Concrete structures that support the foundation walls. They should be twice the width of those walls.

foundation
The structure that bears the weight of the house and holds back the earth around it. Usually dug at least 4 feet below the frost line, foundations are made of hard, durable materials such as stone, brick, and various forms of concrete.

G

gable
The triangular upper part of a wall formed where two sloping surfaces of a roof meet.

gable vent
A louvered opening in the top of a gable designed to ventilate the attic.

geothermal system
A heating and cooling system that takes advantage of the earth's consistent temperature. Geothermal systems can replace more traditional home heating and cooling methods.

GFCI
Ground-fault circuit interrupter, an automatic switch that cuts power to a receptacle if it detects leakage of electricity from the intended path or circuit. That leaking electricity may be flowing through a person, and the GFCI cuts power to protect against shock or electrocution. GFCIs are required for outside outlets, and those serving kitchen counters, in bathrooms, in garages, unfinished basements, and other places.

grade
Also gradient, the slope of an area of land.

H

home inspector
A person who, independently or in association with a small or nationwide home inspection company, inspects homes to assist potential buyers in making real estate decisions. Services usually include the inspection and a written report, and are charged on either a flat-rate or an hourly basis.

HVAC
The heating, ventilation, and air-conditioning systems of a house.

I

ice dam
A buildup of ice at the edge of a roof that prevents water from draining into the gutters, causing the water to back up under the shingles and possibly into the interior.

insulated concrete forms (ICF)
Foam blocks reinforced with metal that are filled with concrete as a wall is built, creating a very strong structure with built-in insulation. ICFs can be used as foundation walls, or for entire structures.

insulbrick
An exterior siding made of asphalt sheathing similar to shingles, printed to look like brick.

J

joists
The wooden boards that stretch from one exterior wall to another (or from an exterior wall to a column or wall in the center), supporting the floor above.

junction box
A five-sided box, typically of PVC plastic or of steel, fiberglass, or cast zinc, that contains electrical connections (junctions or splices) to protect them from damage, and to contain heat or sparks if the junctions fail. Any junction box has to have a proper cover installed on it to fully enclose the splices.

K

knob-and-tube wiring
The oldest form of electrical wiring, in which wires were strung through insulating ceramic knobs and tubes (the latter used when the wires passed through joists or studs).

M

MDF
Medium-density fiberboard, made of wood fibers (sawdust) bonded by an adhesive and pressed into sheets often used for kitchen and bathroom cabinets as well as for other built-ins and shelving.

O

OSB
Oriented strand board, a modern version of plywood that uses layers of wood flakes, fibers, or strands bonded together under intense heat and pressure. The direction of the fibers alternates between layers for greater strength.

P

parging
A thin layer of cement or mortar used to cover a masonry wall to improve moisture protection or create a smoother surface.

pitch
The ratio between the vertical (rise) and horizontal (run) dimensions of a roof.

property inspector
A home inspector who specializes in commercial buildings.

R

repointing
A method of repairing damaged brickwork by chiseling out cracked or crumbling mortar and replacing it.

rise and run
See pitch.

roof vent
A covered opening in the roof that is designed to ventilate the attic.

S

slab-on-grade
A type of foundation in which concrete is poured over insulation and gravel directly on the ground (that is, there is no basement).

soffits
The undersides of the roof eaves that are visible from the ground. Modern soffits are perforated to allow for air movement in and out of the attic.

stucco
Traditionally a mixture of Portland cement, sand, lime, and water used for covering exterior walls. Newer stucco compounds are less porous.

T

thermal barrier
A material (such as rigid foam) used between warm areas (such as the interior of a house) and cold areas (such as the exterior, in northern climates) to lessen moisture buildup and heat loss.

thermal break
A material (such as foam) that completely separates warm areas (such as the interior of a house) from cold areas (such as the exterior, in northern climates). Because warm and cold do not meet at all, there is no moisture buildup or heat loss. The best analogy is the structure of a beverage cooler: the built-in foam insulation acts as a thermal break to keep cold drinks completely separated from the warm air outside.

thermographic imaging
A process that captures heat differences between various surfaces by measuring infrared radiation.

V

vapor barrier
Usually a sheet of 6-mil polyethylene plastic stapled to the studs on the warm side of an exterior wall (on top of the insulation) to prevent water vapor from forming inside the walls.

vent stack
Also called a waste stack, a vertical pipe that carries waste products from the plumbing system down and out to the municipal sewer or septic system. It also vents noxious odors and gases through a pipe that exits the house through and extending above the roof. The pipe also allows air to enter the waste system, allowing it to drain quickly.

W

water table
The level below which the ground is saturated with water. The level of the water table varies from place to place and at different times of the year.

ACKNOWLEDGEMENTS

I have always thought of myself as a contractor. It's my passion for contracting that has made it possible for me to become a television host, a philanthropist, an advocate, a teacher, a home builder, and a writer of books. That passion was first ignited by my dad. He's the one who challenged me to make it right—the first time. If only I could thank him for that gift today.

In the years since my dad died, my passion for the trades has been encouraged by those I interact with. I've always said that you're only as good as the people around you. And so, like everything I do, this book reflects those talented people who have helped take my words and ideas and shape them into the book you are holding now.

Many of those ideas start with one-on-one meetings with people on the street, at the airport, in schools, or at home shows. They are conversations with homeowners, skilled contractors, architects, real estate agents, and of course, home inspectors. If I've had one of those conversations with you, thank you. I love getting your questions and support. Because it helps me learn more about why residential construction needs to be fixed, and how this can be done.

I get tens of thousands of homeowners writing to me every year with angry, scary, and tragic stories. But all too often those stories start with a home inspection that went wrong. Hopefully this book will help fix that problem so that everyone involved in the home buying and selling process will be more aware, ask more questions, and demand more value. Maybe then we can put more focus on building better homes. Remember, build it right the first time. So a special thank you to everyone who let me use excerpts from their letters in this book.

A big thank you to my team. Whether the crew in the field or the gang in the office, you often go way beyond the call and I know that you always put in a 110 percent effort.

Special thanks to HarperCollins Canada and especially Brad Wilson and Nicole Langlois for their experience, patience, and passion; to Liza Drozdov for her keen eye and challenging questions; and to my left and right hands, Michael Quast and Pete Kettlewell, whose tireless efforts and support can be found on every page of this book.

The greatest appreciation and gratitude goes to my family—with special mention to Anna, Uncle Billy, Sherry, Mike Jr., and Amanda. You keep me grounded and real. I love you all.

And finally, a last thank you to you, the reader. I hope this book helps you find a safe, comfortable, and sound house that you can call home.

INDEX